The OXFORD JUNIOR ATLAS

Acknowledgements

The Publisher would like to thank the following for
permission to reproduce photographs:
Aerofilms p.6; Airviews Ltd p.7;
Bryan and Cherry Alexander p.41;
Ardea pp.34, 39;
Australian Information Service/London p.39;
Barnabys Picture Library pp.6, 34;
BBC Hulton Picture Library p.47; Douglas Botting p.29;
Camerapix Hutchison pp.21, 37, 43;
J Allan Cash pp.7, 20, 23, 29, 35, 37, 41, 43,
44, 48 and cover; Ben Crow p. 50;
Bruce Coleman Ltd p.7; Colorific pp.38, 39, 43;
Colour Library International pp. 7, 23, 35, 50;
Daily Telegraph Colour Library pp.34, 45, 47;
James Davis Photography p.6; Douglas Dickins p.29;
Patrick Eagar p.44; Robert Estall pp.6, 23; Fiat p.31;
Geoscience Features p.29;
Robert Harding Associates pp.21, 29, 46;
John Hillelson p.29; Interfoto Archives pp.6, 7;
Image Bank p.46; Rob Judges p.9; Eric Kay p.6;
Mansell Collection p.47;
Mountain Camera/John Cleare p.20;
National Remote Sensing Centre/Farnborough pp.4, 5;
Picturepoint pp.6, 20, 22, 29, 39; G R Roberts p.38;
Arthur Shepherd p.21; Adrian Smith p.20
South American Pictures/Tony Morrison p.43;
Spectrum Colour Library p.22; Frank Spooner Pictures p.49;
Jenny Thomas p.6; John Topham p.29;
Vision International pp.29, 41, 49; Patrick Wiegand p.21;
Zefa pp.23, 30, 38, 41, 46, 48, 49 and cover.

The illustrations are by Bob Chapman, Peter Connolly,
Roger Gorringe, Gordon Lawson, Jon Riley, and
Bernard Robinson.

Pages 11 and 12 are based upon the 1981 Ordnance
Survey 1:250,000 Routemaster maps with the permission
of the Controller of Her Majesty's Stationery Office. Crown
copyright reserved.

Oxford London
New York Toronto Melbourne Auckland
Kuala Lumpur Singapore Hong Kong Tokyo
Delhi Bombay Calcutta Madras Karachi
Nairobi Dar es Salaam Cape Town
and associated companies in
Beirut Berlin Ibadan Mexico City Nicosia

Oxford is a trade mark of Oxford University Press

ISBN 0 19 831655 0 (non net) ISBN 0 19 831656 9 (hardback)

Printed in Hong Kong

Editorial Adviser
Patrick Wiegand

Oxford University Press

Contents

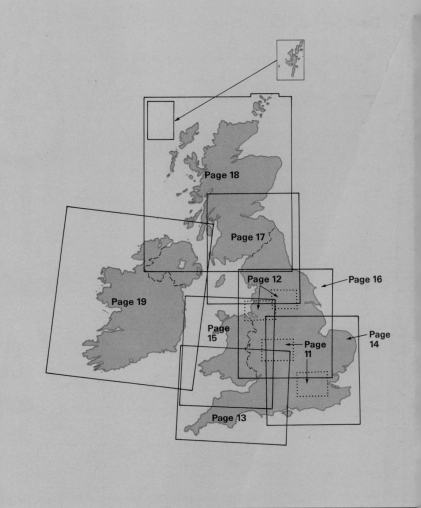

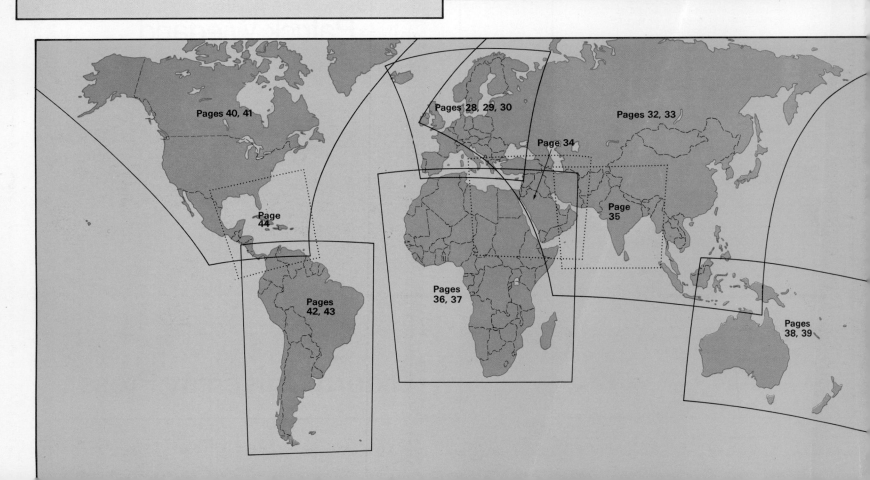

Continents, Countries and Capitals

Use this page to find countries and capital cities on the atlas maps

France   The names of countries are shown in this colour

Paris   The names of capital cities are shown in this colour

Europe

Albania	Tiranë
Andorra	Andorra la Vella
Austria	Vienna
Belgium	Brussels
Bulgaria	Sofiya
Cyprus	Nicosia
Czechoslovakia	Prague
Denmark	Copenhagen
East Germany	East Berlin
Finland	Helsinki
France	Paris
Greece	Athens
Hungary	Budapest
Iceland	Reykjavik
Irish Republic	Dublin
Italy	Rome
Liechtenstein	Vaduz
Luxembourg	Luxembourg
Malta	Valletta
Monaco	Monaco-Ville
Netherlands	Amsterdam
Norway	Oslo
Poland	Warsaw
Portugal	Lisbon
Romania	Bucharest
San Marino	San Marino
Spain	Madrid
Sweden	Stockholm
Switzerland	Bern
Turkey	Ankara
United Kingdom	London
West Germany	Bonn
Yugoslavia	Belgrade

North America

Bahamas	Nassau
Barbados	Bridgetown
Belize	Belmopan
Canada	Ottawa
Costa Rica	San José
Cuba	Havana
Dominica	Roseau
Dominican Republic	
	Santo Domingo
El Salvador	San Salvador
Greenland	Nuuk
Guatemala	Guatemala
Haiti	Port-aû-Prince
Honduras	Tegucigalpa
Jamaica	Kingston
Mexico	Mexico City
Nicaragua	Managua
Panama	Panamá
Puerto Rico	San Juan
Trinidad and Tobago	Port of Spain
United States of America	
	Washington D.C.

Africa

Algeria	Algiers
Angola	Luanda
Benin	Porto Novo
Botswana	Gaborone
Burkina Faso	Ouagadougou
Burundi	Bujumbura
Cameroun	Yaoundé
Cape Verde Islands	Praia
Central African Republic	Bangui
Chad	N'Djamena
Comoro Islands	Moroni
Congo	Brazzaville
Djibouti	Djibouti
Egypt	Cairo
Equatorial Guinea	Malabo
Ethiopia	Addis Ababa
Gabon	Libreville
Gambia	Banjul
Ghana	Accra
Guinea	Conakry
Guinea-Bissau	Bissau
Ivory Coast	Abidjan
Kenya	Nairobi
Lesotho	Maseru
Liberia	Monrovia
Libya	Tripoli
Madagascar	Antananarivo
Malawi	Lilongwe
Mali	Bamako
Mauritania	Nouakchott
Morocco	Rabat
Mozambique	Maputo
Namibia	Windhoek
Niger	Niamey
Nigeria	Lagos
Rwanda	Kigali
São Tomé and Principe	São Tomé
Sierra Leone	Freetown
Somali Republic	Mogadiscio
South Africa	Cape Town, and Pretoria
Sudan	Khartoum
Swaziland	Mbabane
Tanzania	Dodoma
Togo	Lomé
Tunisia	Tunis
Uganda	Kampala
Zaire	Kinshasa
Zambia	Lusaka
Zimbabwe	Harare

Asia

Afghanistan	Kabul
Bahrain	Manama
Bangladesh	Dacca
Bhutan	Thimpu
Brunei	Bandar Seri Begawan
Burma	Rangoon
Cambodia (Kampuchea)	
	Phnom Penh
China	Peking
India	Delhi
Indonesia	Jakarta
Iran	Tehran
Iraq	Baghdad
Israel	Jerusalem
Hong Kong	Victoria
Japan	Tokyo
Jordan	Amman
Kuwait	Kuwait
Laos	Vientiane
Lebanon	Beirut
Malaysia	Kuala Lumpur
Nepal	Katmandu
North Korea	Pyongyang
Oman	Muscat
Pakistan	Islamabad
Philippines	Manila
Qatar	Doha
Saudi Arabia	Riyadh
Singapore	Singapore
South Korea	Seoul
South Yemen	Aden
Sri Lanka	Colombo
Syria	Damascus
Taiwan	Taipei
Thailand	Bangkok
Union of Soviet Socialist Republics	
	Moscow
United Arab Emirates	Abu Dhabi
Vietnam	Hanoi
Yemen	San'a

Australasia

Australia	Canberra
Fiji	Suva
Kiribati	Bairiki
Nauru	Domaneab
New Zealand	Wellington
Papua-New Guinea	Port Moresby
Solomon Islands	Honiara
Tonga	Nuku'alofa
Tuvalu	Funafuti
Vanuatu	Vila
Western Samoa	Apia

South America

Argentina	Buenos Aires
Bolivia	La Paz
Brazil	Brasília
Chile	Santiago
Colombia	Bogotá
Ecuador	Quito
French Guiana	Cayenne
Guyana	Georgetown
Paraguay	Asunción
Peru	Lima
Surinam	Paramaribo
Uruguay	Montevideo
Venezuela	Caracas

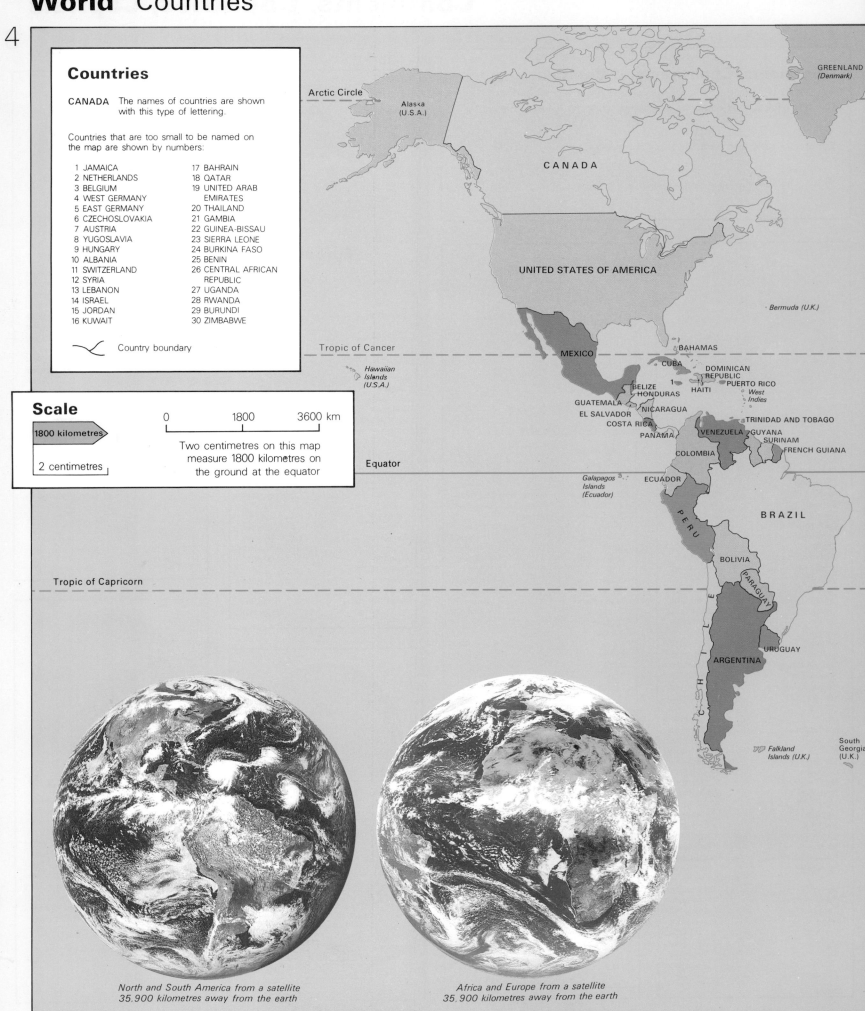

Countries

CANADA The names of countries are shown with this type of lettering.

Countries that are too small to be named on the map are shown by numbers:

1 JAMAICA	17 BAHRAIN
2 NETHERLANDS	18 QATAR
3 BELGIUM	19 UNITED ARAB
4 WEST GERMANY	EMIRATES
5 EAST GERMANY	20 THAILAND
6 CZECHOSLOVAKIA	21 GAMBIA
7 AUSTRIA	22 GUINEA-BISSAU
8 YUGOSLAVIA	23 SIERRA LEONE
9 HUNGARY	24 BURKINA FASO
10 ALBANIA	25 BENIN
11 SWITZERLAND	26 CENTRAL AFRICAN
12 SYRIA	REPUBLIC
13 LEBANON	27 UGANDA
14 ISRAEL	28 RWANDA
15 JORDAN	29 BURUNDI
16 KUWAIT	30 ZIMBABWE

‿ Country boundary

Scale

1800 kilometres ➤

2 centimetres

0   1800   3600 km

Two centimetres on this map measure 1800 kilometres on the ground at the equator

Arctic Circle

GREENLAND (Denmark)

Alaska (U.S.A.)

CANADA

UNITED STATES OF AMERICA

Bermuda (U.K.)

Tropic of Cancer

MEXICO

BAHAMAS

CUBA

DOMINICAN REPUBLIC

PUERTO RICO

Hawaiian Islands (U.S.A.)

1

BELIZE

HONDURAS

HAITI

West Indies

GUATEMALA

EL SALVADOR

NICARAGUA

COSTA RICA

TRINIDAD AND TOBAGO

PANAMA

VENEZUELA

GUYANA

SURINAM

COLOMBIA

FRENCH GUIANA

Equator

Galapagos Islands (Ecuador)

ECUADOR

P E R U

B R A Z I L

BOLIVIA

Tropic of Capricorn

PARAGUAY

C H I L E

URUGUAY

ARGENTINA

Falkland Islands (U.K.)

South Georgia (U.K.)

North and South America from a satellite 35,900 kilometres away from the earth

Africa and Europe from a satellite 35,900 kilometres away from the earth

ICELAND

Faeroe Islands (Denmark)

NORWAY

SWEDEN

FINLAND

UNION OF SOVIET SOCIALIST REPUBLICS

IRISH REPUBLIC

UNITED KINGDOM

DENMARK

2

3

4

5 POLAND

6

7

8

9

11

FRANCE

ITALY

10

ROMANIA

BULGARIA

MONGOLIA

NORTH KOREA

SOUTH KOREA

JAPAN

PORTUGAL SPAIN

GREECE

TURKEY

AFGHANISTAN

CHINA

Canary Islands (Spain)

MOROCCO

TUNISIA

CYPRUS 13 12

14

15

16

IRAQ

IRAN

PAKISTAN

NEPAL

BHUTAN

TAIWAN

Tropic of Cancer

ALGERIA

LIBYA

EGYPT

17

18

19

SAUDI ARABIA

OMAN

INDIA

BURMA

Hong Kong (U.K.)

MAURITANIA

MALI

NIGER

CHAD

SUDAN

YEMEN

SOUTH YEMEN

Socotra (South Yemen)

BANGLADESH

LAOS

VIETNAM

PHILIPPINES

SENEGAL

21

22

GUINEA

23

LIBERIA

24

25

GHANA

NIGERIA

DJIBOUTI

ETHIOPIA

SRI LANKA

20

KAMPUCHEA

BRUNEI

MALAYSIA

IVORY COAST

TOGO

26

CAMEROUN

SOMALI REPUBLIC

SINGAPORE

Equator

EQUATORIAL GUINEA

GABON

CONGO

ZAÏRE

28

29

27

KENYA

TANZANIA

INDONESIA

PAPUA-NEW GUINEA

SOLOMON ISLANDS

ANGOLA

ZAMBIA

MALAWI

MOZAMBIQUE

MADAGASCAR

MAURITIUS

Réunion (France)

VANUATU

FIJI

New Caledonia (France)

NAMIBIA

30

BOTSWANA

SWAZILAND

Tropic of Capricorn

AUSTRALIA

SOUTH AFRICA

LESOTHO

NEW ZEALAND

Italy from a satellite 1450 kilometres away from the earth.

Naples and Mount Vesuvius from a satellite 1450 kilometres away from the earth.

Roads, rivers and towns fit together like the pieces in a jigsaw puzzle. On these two pages you can see some of the features that make up the countryside. They are shown on the map by **symbols**. These symbols are the ones used for the maps on pages 11 to 19. Can you find each of the places shown here on the maps ?

Symbols

– – –	national boundary
– –	county boundary
▪▪▪▪▪▪	motorways
⌒⌒	other main roads
⟩	railway
⌐⌐	canal
✈	main airport
⌇	river
⬮	lake
▲	peak or highest point
◈	largest built-up areas

Towns

■	largest towns
●	large towns
•	other towns

The photograph on the right shows the area marked with a square on the map above.

Llanfairfechan, Page 15 H5

Boundaries

 national boundary

Boundaries mark the edges between one type of land and another. National boundaries show where one country ends and another begins.

Sign marking the boundary between Wales and England near Hay-on-Wye, Page 15 H4

– – county boundary

County boundaries mark the places where counties meet.

River Dove forming the boundary between Derbyshire and Staffordshire, Page 16 K5

Communications

▪▪▪▪▪▪ motorways

Motorways are shown separately on the maps because they are important for the fast movement of passengers and goods.

A102(M) in east London, Page 11

⌒⌒ other main roads

Other main roads are shown but not small ones. Only the road in the centre of the picture would be shown on the maps in this atlas.

A423 between Banbury and Oxford, Page 14 K3

⟩ railway

Main line routes are marked on the map but not small goods lines.

Main line between Swansea and London near Bath, Page 13 J3

⌐⌐ canal

Busy canals in the main built-up areas are shown on page 11 and 12 only.

Leeds and Liverpool Canal at Skipton, Page 12

✈ main airport

Only the airports that have regular flights to other countries are shown.

Manchester International Airport, Page 16 J5

Rivers and Peaks

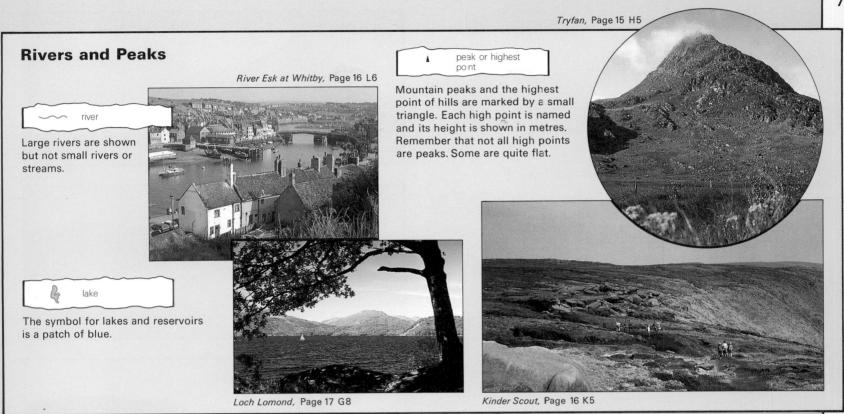

Tryfan, Page 15 H5

River Esk at Whitby, Page 16 L6

| ⌁ | river |

Large rivers are shown but not small rivers or streams.

| ▲ | peak or highest point |

Mountain peaks and the highest point of hills are marked by a small triangle. Each high point is named and its height is shown in metres. Remember that not all high points are peaks. Some are quite flat.

| 🝆 | lake |

The symbol for lakes and reservoirs is a patch of blue.

Loch Lomond, Page 17 G8

Kinder Scout, Page 16 K5

Towns

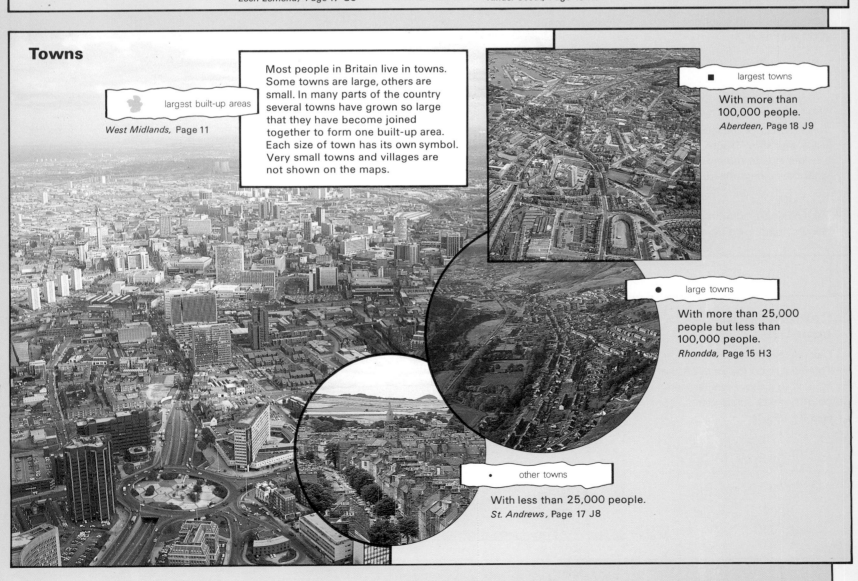

| 🝆 | largest built-up areas |

West Midlands, Page 11

Most people in Britain live in towns. Some towns are large, others are small. In many parts of the country several towns have grown so large that they have become joined together to form one built-up area. Each size of town has its own symbol. Very small towns and villages are not shown on the maps.

| ■ | largest towns |

With more than 100,000 people.
Aberdeen, Page 18 J9

| ● | large towns |

With more than 25,000 people but less than 100,000 people.
Rhondda, Page 15 H3

| • | other towns |

With less than 25,000 people.
St. Andrews, Page 17 J8

Colours show height

All the atlas maps are in colour.
The colours may mean different things.
Often they show how high the land is.
Some land in this view is high, other land is low.

Here is the same view.
Lines have been drawn on the picture.
All the places along the 100–metre line are 100 metres high.
All the places along the 500–metre line are 500 metres high.
Lines like this are called **contours**.

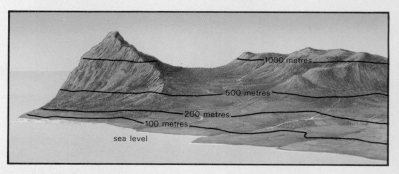

Now the gaps between the contours have been coloured.

All the land coloured like this  is between 100 metres and 200 metres high.

All the land in this colour is between 500 and 1000 metres high.

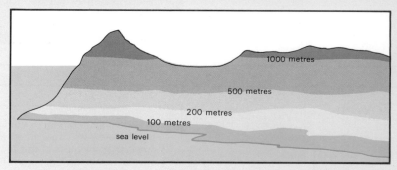

This is a map of the same place.
Maps that show height have
a colour box to remind you
what the colours mean.

Take care! On some maps the
colours stand for different heights.

Land Height

Measured above Sea Level

More than 1000 metres

500–1000 metres

200–500 metres

100–200 metres

Less than 100 metres

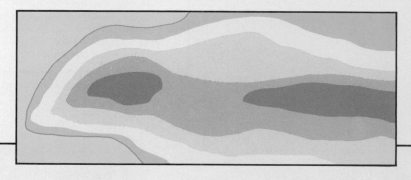

Colours show countries

Colours can mean other things too.
The colours on the map on the
right simply show where one
country ends and another
country begins.

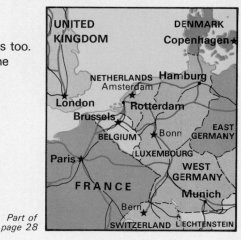

*Part of
page 28*

Colours show environments

This map uses colour to
show what the land is like.
It is an **environment** map.
Colours on these maps are
explained by photographs
which show what you might
see if you went there.

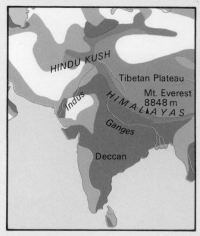

*Part of
page 33*

A globe is a model of the world. It is much smaller than the planet itself. Maps have to be smaller than the countries they show. You could not have a piece of paper the size of a country. That would be impossible! A few centimetres on the map have to stand for many kilometres on the ground.

Every map in this atlas has a sign like this:

> 25 kilometres
> 2 centimetres

2 centimetres on a map with *this* sign would stand for 25 kilometres on the ground.

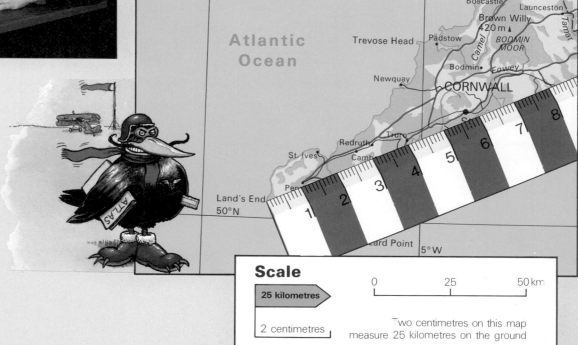

The crow is going to fly from Land's End to Truro.

On the map his journey measures 4 centimetres.

He will have to fly a distance of 50 kilometres.

Scale

> 25 kilometres
>
> 2 centimetres

0   25   50 km

Two centimetres on this map measure 25 kilometres on the ground

Several different **scales** are used for maps in this atlas. Here are some of them shown side by side.

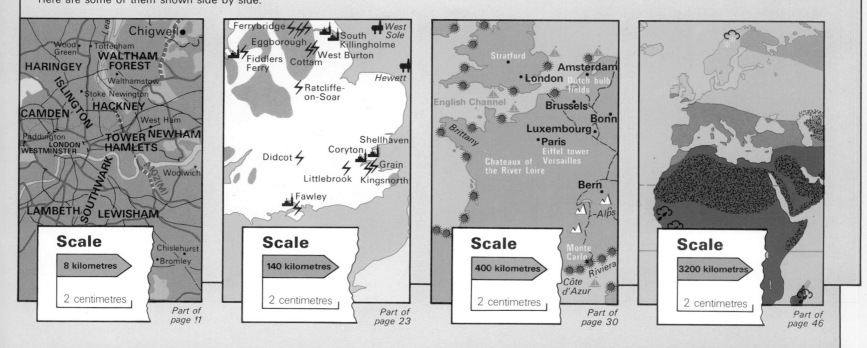

Scale

> 8 kilometres
>
> 2 centimetres

Part of page 11

Scale

> 140 kilometres
>
> 2 centimetres

Part of page 23

Scale

> 400 kilometres
>
> 2 centimetres

Part of page 30

Scale

> 3200 kilometres
>
> 2 centimetres

Part of page 46

British Isles

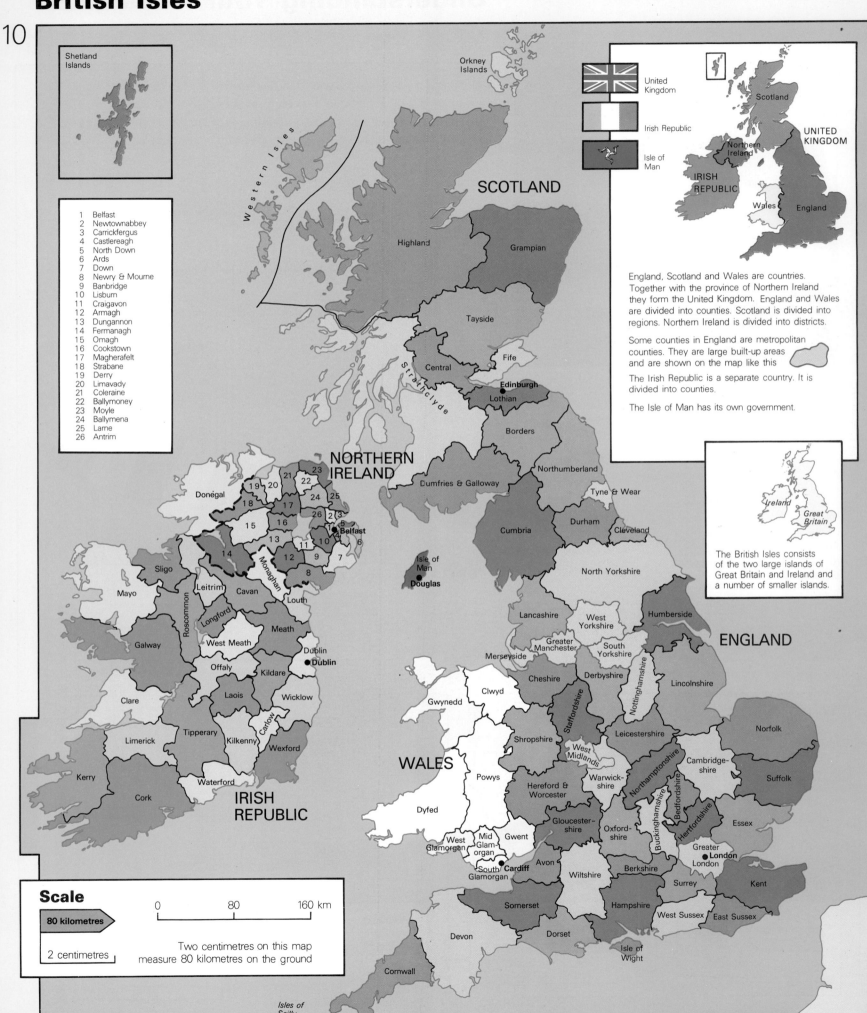

Shetland Islands

1 Belfast
2 Newtownabbey
3 Carrickfergus
4 Castlereagh
5 North Down
6 Ards
7 Down
8 Newry & Mourne
9 Banbridge
10 Lisburn
11 Craigavon
12 Armagh
13 Dungannon
14 Fermanagh
15 Omagh
16 Cookstown
17 Magherafelt
18 Strabane
19 Derry
20 Limavady
21 Coleraine
22 Ballymoney
23 Moyle
24 Ballymena
25 Larne
26 Antrim

United Kingdom

Irish Republic

Isle of Man

England, Scotland and Wales are countries.
Together with the province of Northern Ireland
they form the United Kingdom. England and Wales
are divided into counties. Scotland is divided into
regions. Northern Ireland is divided into districts.

Some counties in England are metropolitan
counties. They are large built-up areas
and are shown on the map like this

The Irish Republic is a separate country. It is
divided into counties.

The Isle of Man has its own government.

UNITED KINGDOM

Scotland

Northern Ireland

IRISH REPUBLIC

Wales

England

Ireland

Great Britain

The British Isles consists
of the two large islands of
Great Britain and Ireland and
a number of smaller islands.

Orkney Islands

Western Isles

SCOTLAND

Highland

Grampian

Tayside

Fife

Central

Strathclyde

Edinburgh
Lothian

Borders

NORTHERN IRELAND

Donegal

Dumfries & Galloway

Northumberland

Tyne & Wear

Durham

Cleveland

Cumbria

Lancashire

North Yorkshire

Humberside

West Yorkshire

Greater Manchester

South Yorkshire

Merseyside

Derbyshire

Lincolnshire

Nottinghamshire

Cheshire

Belfast

Isle of Man

Douglas

Sligo

Leitrim

Cavan

Monaghan

Louth

Mayo

Roscommon

Longford

West Meath

Meath

Galway

Offaly

Kildare

Dublin

Dublin

Wicklow

Clare

Laois

Carlow

Limerick

Tipperary

Kilkenny

Wexford

Kerry

Waterford

Cork

IRISH REPUBLIC

WALES

Gwynedd

Clwyd

Powys

Dyfed

Shropshire

Staffordshire

West Midlands

Warwickshire

Leicestershire

Northamptonshire

Cambridgeshire

Norfolk

Suffolk

Hereford & Worcester

West Glamorgan

Mid Glamorgan

Gwent

Gloucestershire

Oxfordshire

Buckinghamshire

Bedfordshire

Hertfordshire

Essex

ENGLAND

South Glamorgan

Cardiff

Avon

Wiltshire

Berkshire

Surrey

Greater London

London

Kent

Somerset

Hampshire

West Sussex

East Sussex

Devon

Dorset

Isle of Wight

Cornwall

Isles of Scilly

Scale

80 kilometres

2 centimetres

0   80   160 km

Two centimetres on this map
measure 80 kilometres on the ground

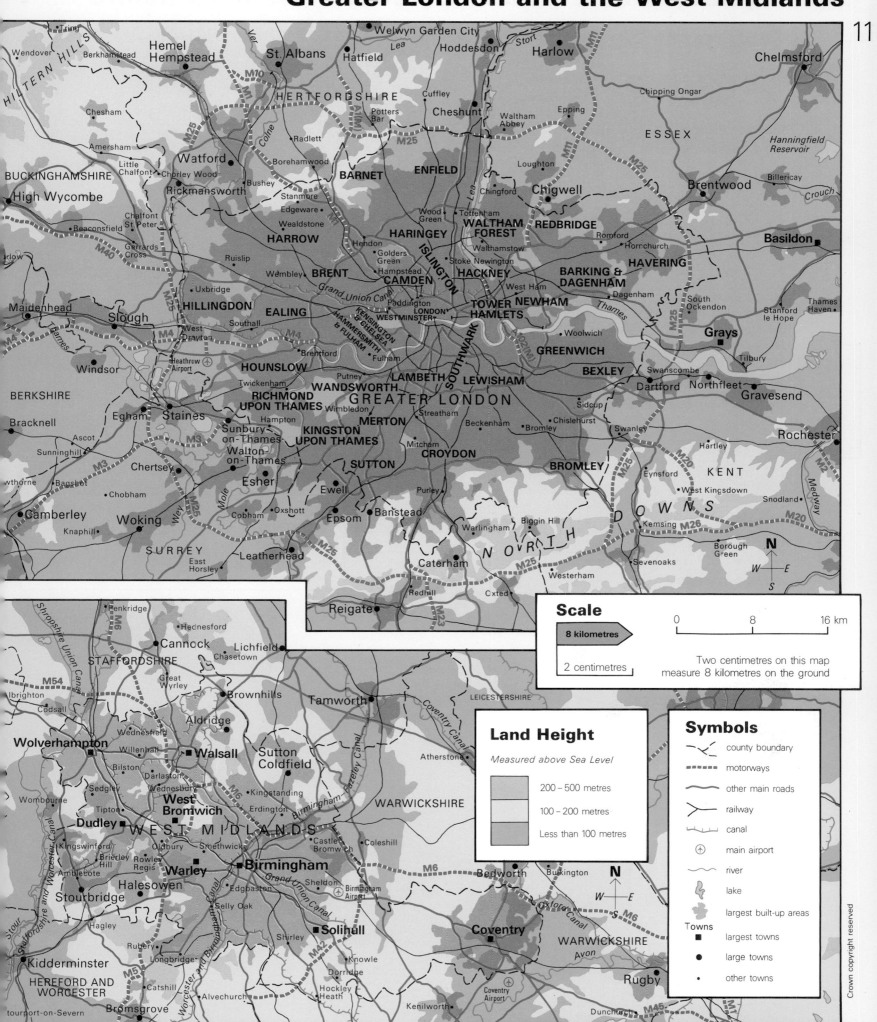

Greater London and the West Midlands

Scale

8 kilometres

2 centimetres

0   8   16 km

Two centimetres on this map
measure 8 kilometres on the ground

Land Height

Measured above Sea Level

200 – 500 metres

100 – 200 metres

Less than 100 metres

Symbols

county boundary

motorways

other main roads

railway

canal

main airport

river

lake

largest built-up areas

Towns

largest towns

large towns

other towns

Merseyside, Greater Manchester and West Yorkshire

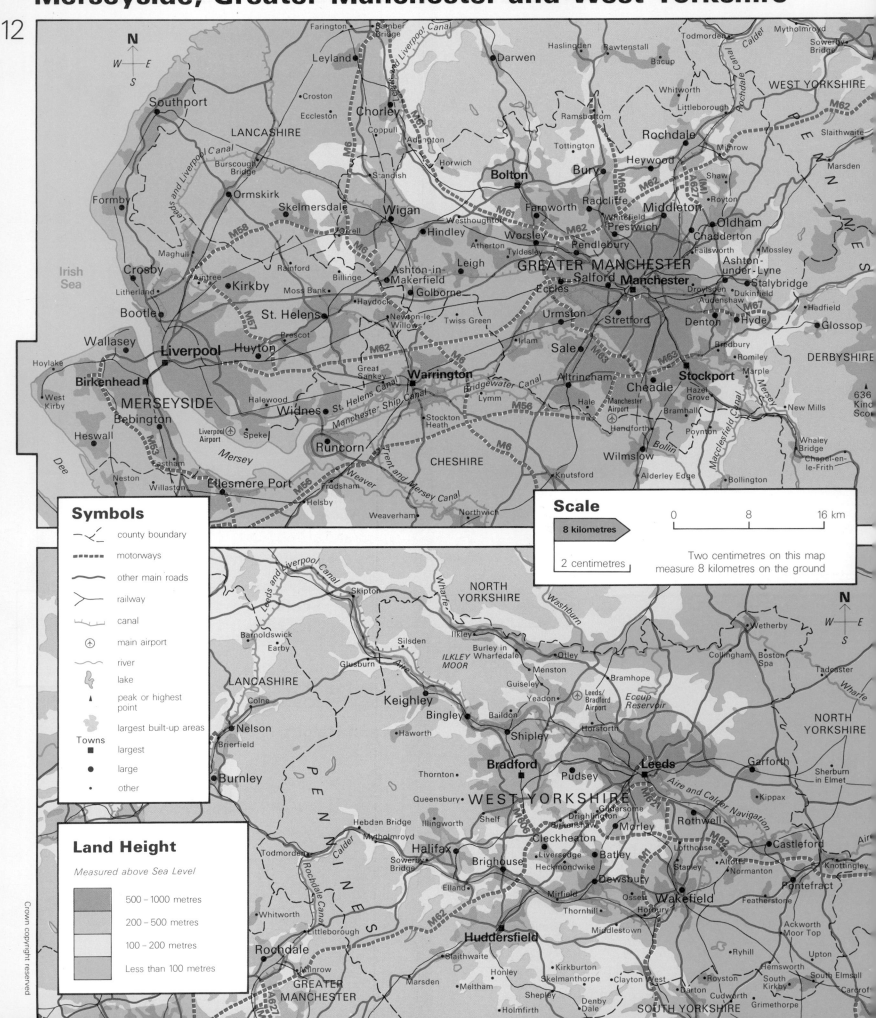

Symbols

- ⌇⌇ county boundary
- ▪▪▪▪ motorways
- ⌒⌒ other main roads
- ⊣⊢ railway
- ⌄⌄ canal
- ⊕ main airport
- ∿∿ river
- lake
- ▲ peak or highest point
- largest built-up areas

Towns
- ■ largest
- ● large
- · other

Scale

0	8	16 km

8 kilometres

2 centimetres

Two centimetres on this map measure 8 kilometres on the ground

Land Height

Measured above Sea Level

- 500 – 1000 metres
- 200 – 500 metres
- 100 – 200 metres
- Less than 100 metres

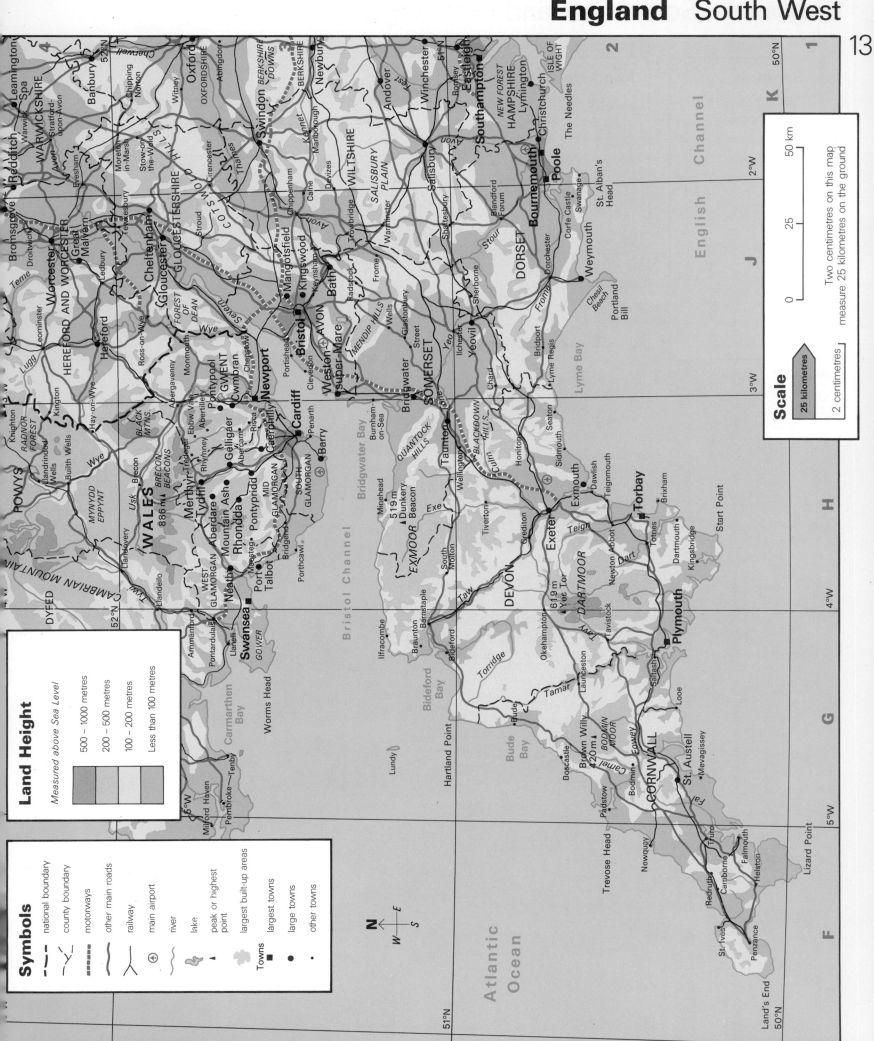

Scale

0   25   50 km

Two centimetres on this map
measure 25 kilometres on the ground

25 kilometres

2 centimetres

Land Height

Measured above Sea Level

500 – 1000 metres
200 – 500 metres
100 – 200 metres
Less than 100 metres

Symbols

national boundary
county boundary
motorways
other main roads
railway
main airport
river
lake
peak or highest point
largest built-up areas

Towns

largest towns
large towns
other towns

N
W — E
S

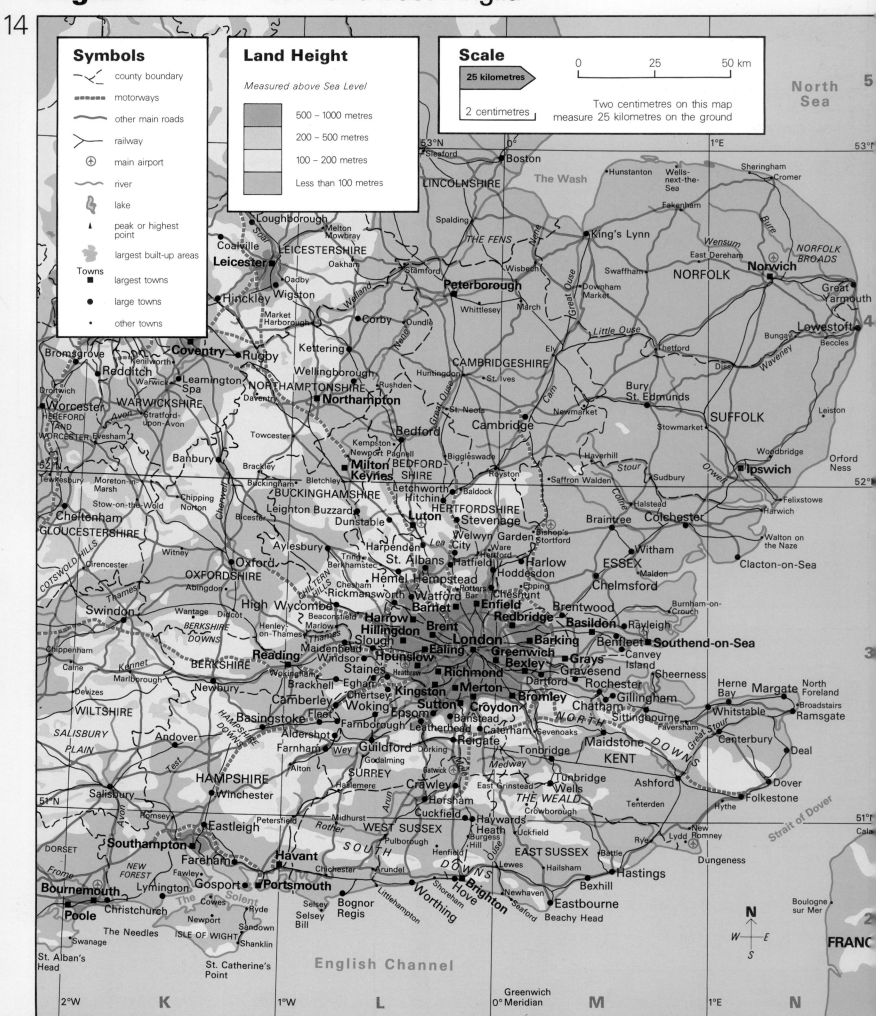

Symbols

county boundary
motorways
other main roads
railway
main airport
river
lake
peak or highest point
largest built-up areas

Towns

■	largest towns
●	large towns
•	other towns

Land Height

Measured above Sea Level

500 – 1000 metres

200 – 500 metres

100 – 200 metres

Less than 100 metres

Scale

25 kilometres

2 centimetres

0   25   50 km

Two centimetres on this map
measure 25 kilometres on the ground

North Sea

53°N   0°   1°E   53°

Sleaford   Boston

The Wash   Hunstanton   Wells-next-the-Sea   Sheringham   Cromer

LINCOLNSHIRE   Spalding   THE FENS   Nene   King's Lynn   Wensum   East Dereham   NORFOLK BROADS

Loughborough   Melton Mowbray   Wisbech   Swaffham   NORFOLK   Norwich

Coalville   Soar   LEICESTERSHIRE   Oakham   Stamford   Downham Market   Great Yarmouth

Leicester   Oadby   Whittlesey   March   Bure

Hinckley   Wigston   Peterborough   Little Ouse   Lowestoft

Market Harborough   Corby   Oundle   Welland   Nene   CAMBRIDGESHIRE   Ely   Thetford   Diss   Bungay   Beccles   Waveney

Coventry   Rugby   Kettering   Great Ouse   Huntingdon   St. Ives   Cam   Bury St. Edmunds   SUFFOLK   Leiston

Bromsgrove   Kenilworth   Warwick   Wellingborough   Rushden   St. Neots   Newmarket   Stowmarket

Redditch   Leamington Spa   NORTHAMPTONSHIRE   Bedford   Cambridge   Haverhill   Stour   Woodbridge

Droitwich   Daventry   Northampton   Biggleswade   Royston   Saffron Walden   Sudbury   Orwell   Ipswich   Orford Ness

Worcester   WARWICKSHIRE   Stratford-upon-Avon   Avon   Towcester   Kempston   BEDFORD-SHIRE   St. Neots   Newport Pagnell   52°N   52°

HEREFORD AND WORCESTER   Evesham   Banbury   Brackley   Milton Keynes   Letchworth   Baldock   Colne   Halstead   Felixstowe   Harwich

Tewkesbury   Moreton-in-Marsh   Buckingham   Bletchley   BUCKINGHAMSHIRE   Hitchin   HERTFORDSHIRE   Braintree   Colchester   Walton on the Naze

Cheltenham   Stow-on-the-Wold   Chipping Norton   Leighton Buzzard   Luton   Stevenage   Witham   Clacton-on-Sea

GLOUCESTERSHIRE   Bicester   Dunstable   Welwyn Garden City   Bishop's Stortford   Harlow   ESSEX   Maldon

COTSWOLD HILLS   Cirencester   Witney   Aylesbury   Harpenden   St. Albans   Hatfield   Hertford   Hoddesdon   Chelmsford   Burnham-on-Crouch

Oxford   OXFORDSHIRE   Tring   Berkhamsted   Hemel Hempstead   Epping   Brentwood

Thames   Abingdon   CHILTERN HILLS   Chesham   Rickmansworth   Watford   Potters Bar   Cheshunt   Redbridge   Rayleigh

Swindon   Wantage   Didcot   High Wycombe   Beaconsfield   Barnet   Enfield   Basildon   Benfleet   Southend-on-Sea

BERKSHIRE DOWNS   Henley-on-Thames   Marlow   Harrow   Brent   London   Barking   Canvey Island

Chippenham   Calne   Reading   Maidenhead   Hillingdon   Ealing   Greenwich   Grays   Sheerness

Kennet   BERKSHIRE   Wokingham   Windsor   Slough   Hounslow   Richmond   Bexley   Gravesend   Herne Bay   Margate   North Foreland

Marlborough   Newbury   Bracknell   Staines   Heathrow   Merton   Bromley   Dartford   Rochester   Broadstairs

Devizes   Camberley   Egham   Chertsey   Kingston   Croydon   Chatham   Gillingham   Whitstable   Ramsgate

WILTSHIRE   Basingstoke   Fleet   Woking   Sutton   Banstead   Sevenoaks   NORTH   DOWNS   Sittingbourne   Faversham

SALISBURY PLAIN   Aldershot   Farnborough   Epsom   Leatherhead   Caterham   Maidstone   Canterbury   Deal

Andover   HAMPSHIRE DOWNS   Farnham   Guildford   Dorking   Reigate   Tonbridge   KENT   Great Stour

Test   Wey   Godalming   Gatwick   Medway   Tunbridge Wells   Ashford   Dover

SURREY   Alton   Crawley   East Grinstead   Folkestone

Salisbury   Winchester   Haslemere   Horsham   THE WEALD   Tenterden   Hythe

Romsey   Petersfield   Midhurst   Arun   Cuckfield   Crowborough   Uckfield   Rye   New Romney

DORSET   Eastleigh   Rother   WEST SUSSEX   Haywards Heath   Battle   Dungeness

Frome   Southampton   Fareham   Pulborough   Burgess Hill   Henfield   EAST SUSSEX   Hailsham   Hastings

NEW FOREST   Fawley   Chichester   Arundel   SOUTH   Lewes   Bexhill

Bournemouth   Lymington   Gosport   Havant   Bognor Regis   Littlehampton   Worthing   Shoreham   DOWNS   Newhaven   Eastbourne   Boulogne sur Mer

Poole   Christchurch   Cowes   Solent   Selsey   Hove   Seaford   Beachy Head

The Needles   Newport   Ryde   Sandown   Selsey Bill   Brighton   FRANCE

Swanage   ISLE OF WIGHT   Shanklin

St. Alban's Head   St. Catherine's Point   **English Channel**

N   W   E   S

2°W   K   1°W   L   Greenwich 0° Meridian   M   1°E   N

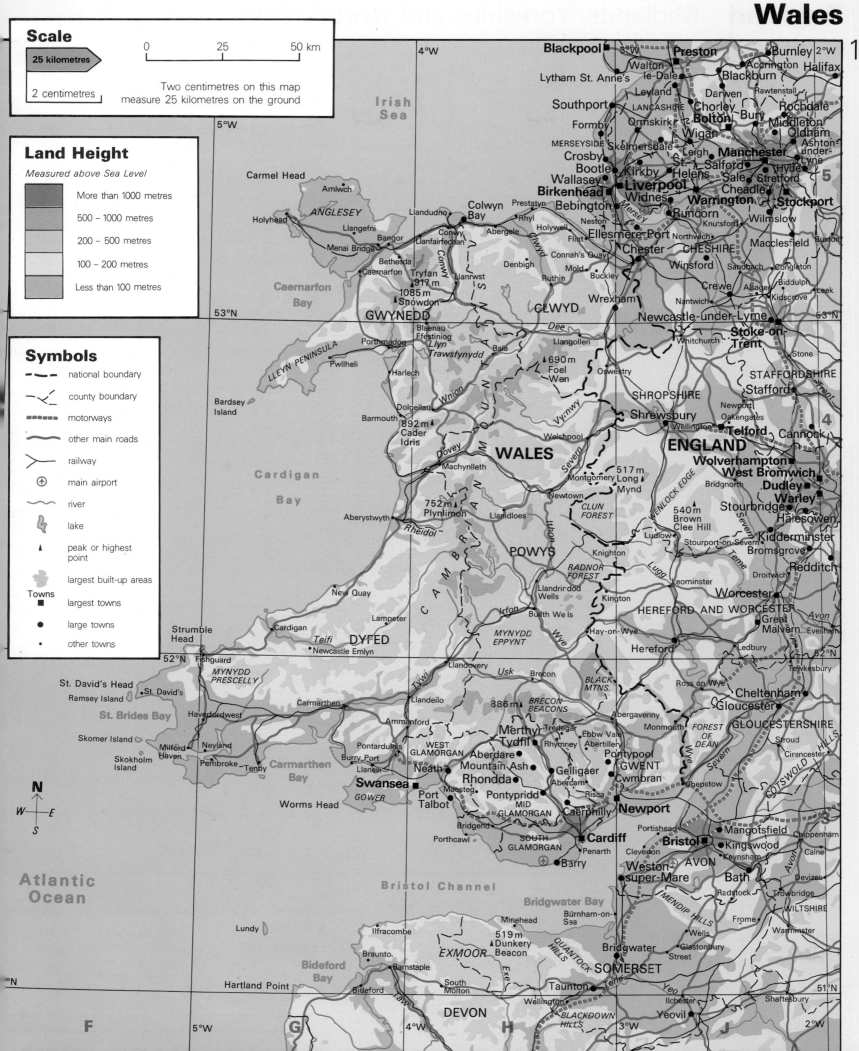

Wales

Scale

25 kilometres

2 centimetres

0   25   50 km

Two centimetres on this map
measure 25 kilometres on the ground

Land Height

Measured above Sea Level

More than 1000 metres

500 – 1000 metres

200 – 500 metres

100 – 200 metres

Less than 100 metres

Symbols

national boundary

county boundary

motorways

other main roads

railway

main airport

river

lake

peak or highest point

largest built-up areas

Towns

largest towns

large towns

other towns

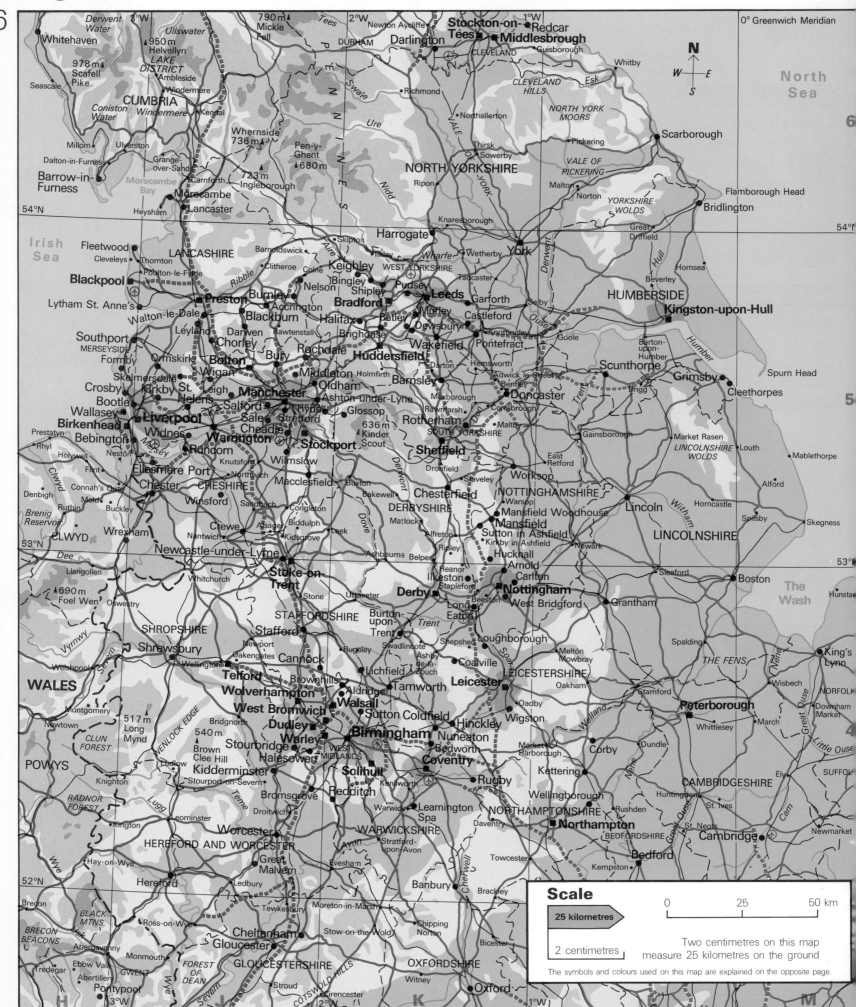

England: Midlands, Yorkshire and North West

Scale

25 kilometres

2 centimetres

0   25   50 km

Two centimetres on this map
measure 25 kilometres on the ground

The symbols and colours used on this map are explained on the opposite page

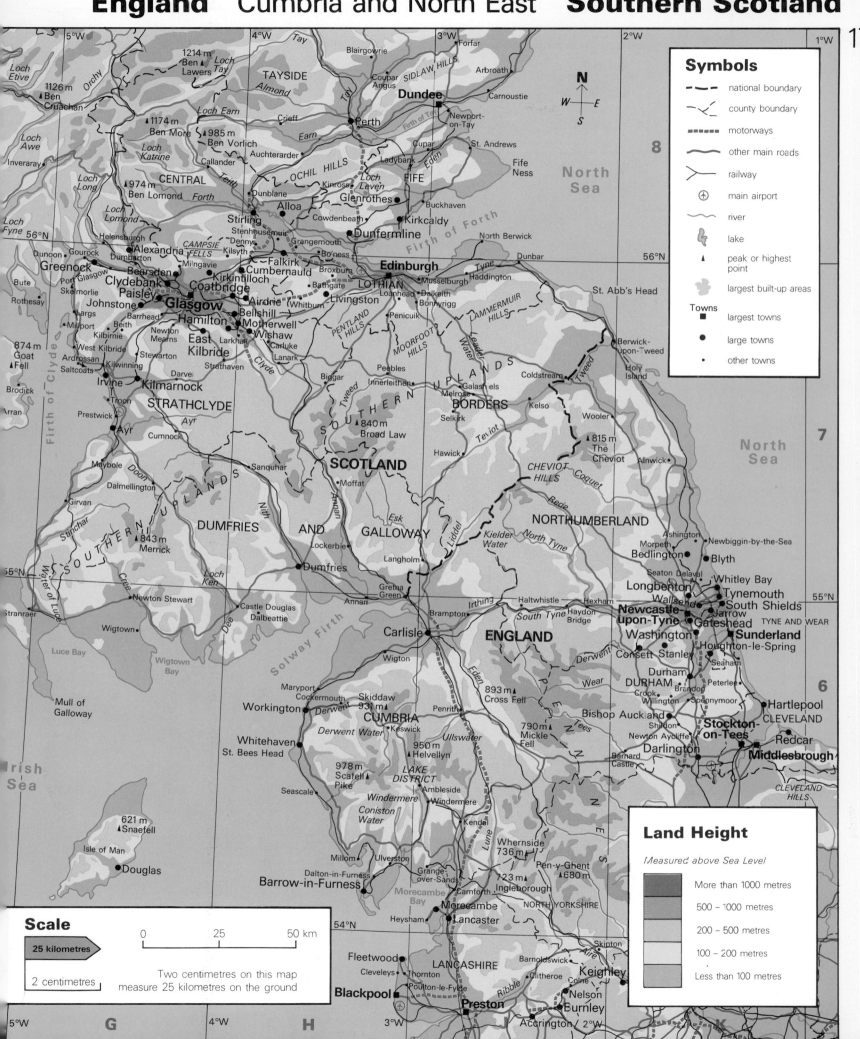

Symbols

- – · – · national boundary
- county boundary
- ------ motorways
- other main roads
- railway
- ⊕ main airport
- river
- lake
- ▲ peak or highest point
- largest built-up areas

Towns

- ■ largest towns
- ● large towns
- · other towns

Land Height

Measured above Sea Level

- More than 1000 metres
- 500 – 1000 metres
- 200 – 500 metres
- 100 – 200 metres
- Less than 100 metres

Scale

25 kilometres

2 centimetres

0 25 50 km

Two centimetres on this map measure 25 kilometres on the ground

Scotland

18

Scale

40 kilometres

2 centimetres

0   40   80 km

Two centimetres on this map
measure 40 kilometres on the ground

The symbols used on this map are explained on the opposite page.

Shetland Islands (inset)

Herma Ness
2°W
Unst
Yell
Fetlar
Out Skerries
Whalsay
St. Magnus Bay
Mainland
Scalloway
Lerwick
Bressay
Foula
60°N
SHETLAND ISLANDS
Sumburgh Head
J   1°W   K   11
12

Main map

3°W Mull Head North Ronaldsay
4°W Papa Westray
Westray
ORKNEY ISLANDS
Rousay Eday Sanday
Stronsay
59°N Mainland Shapinsay
Stromness Kirkwall
Hoy South Ronaldsay
Pentland Firth
Dunnet Head
Duncansby Head
Thurso John o'Groats
Wick
North Sea

Cape Wrath
Butt of Lewis
Stornoway
Lewis
The Minch
927 m ▲ Ben Hope
961 m ▲ Ben Klibreck
998 m Ben More Assynt
Loch Shin
Thurso
Helmsdale
Brora
58°N
Ullapool
Carron
Tarbat Ness
Tain
Clisham 799 m ▲
Harris Scalpay
Pabbay
Berneray
North Uist
Benbecula
WESTERN ISLES
Outer Hebrides
Little Minch
The Storr 719 m ▲
Portree
Skye Raasay
Scalpay
CUILLIN HILLS 1009 m ▲
Kyle of Lochalsh
1081 m Beinn Dearg
1109 m Sgurr Mor
1009 m Beinn Eighe
Ben Wyvis ▲ 1046 m
Meig
Dingwall
Inverness
Elgin Buckie
Nairn
Deveron
Fraserburgh
Peterhead
HIGHLAND
1183 m ▲ Carn Eige
Loch Ness
Beauly
Spey Grantown-on-Spey
Huntly
Inverurie
57°N
South Uist
Eriskay
Canna
Rhum
Barra
Mingulay
Fort Augustus
MONADHLIATH MTNS.
Aviemore
Kingussie
CAIRNGORMS Ben Macdhui ▲ 1310 m
GRAMPIAN
Aberdeen
Don
Dee
Eigg
Muck
Mallaig
Loch Lochy
Fort William
Ben Alder 1148 m ▲
1344 m ▲ Ben Nevis
Loch Shiel
Loch Linnhe
GRAMPIAN MOUNTAINS
FOREST OF ATHOLL
1155 m ▲ Lochnagar
North Esk
South Esk
Ballater
Brechin
Montrose
Stonehaven
Coll
Tiree
Ulva
Mull
Iona
Oban
Loch Awe
Inveraray
Scarba
Loch Rannoch
Loch Tay
1214 m Ben Lawers
Tay
Pitlochry
Isla
TAYSIDE
Blairgowrie
Forfar
Arbroath
1126 m Ben Cruachan
SCOTLAND
1174 m ▲ Ben More
Earn
Crieff
Perth Tay
Dundee
St. Andrews
974 m Ben Lomond
CENTRAL
Auchterarder
LOCHIL HILLS
FIFE
Buckhaven
Glenrothes
Kirkcaldy
Firth of Lorn
Colonsay
Oronsay
56°N
Loch Fyne
Helensburgh
Loch Lomond
Stirling Alloa
Forth
Dunfermline
Falkirk
Edinburgh
North Berwick
Dunbar
Firth of Forth
Musselburgh
LOTHIAN
St. Abb's Head
Jura
Bute
Greenock
Cumbernauld
Clydebank Coatbridge
Paisley Glasgow
Airdrie
Livingston
Penicuik
LAMMERMUIR HILLS
Berwick-upon-Tweed
Holy Island
Sound of Jura
Gigha
Islay
STRATHCLYDE
Motherwell
East Kilbride Hamilton
Lanark
Peebles
Tweed
SOUTHERN UPLANDS
Galashiels
Selkirk
BORDERS
874 m Goat Fell
Arran
Irvine
Kilmarnock
840 m Broad Law
Hawick
815 m The Cheviot
CHEVIOT HILLS
Firth of Clyde
Prestwick
Ayr Ayr
Cumnock
Teviot
Coquet
Mull of Kintyre
Campbeltown
Girvan
Doon
Annan
NORTHUMBERLAND
Ashington
Rathlin Island
Stinchar
Nith
Esk
Liddel
Kielder Water
Bedlington
TYNE AND WEAR
Blyth
55°N
Merrick 843 m ▲
DUMFRIES AND GALLOWAY
Cree
Dumfries
Tyne
Wear
Newcastle-upon-Tyne
Sunderland
ANTRIM MOUNTAINS
Ballymena
Larne
Carrickfergus
NORTHERN IRELAND
Newtownabbey
Belfast
Bangor
Belfast Lough
North Channel
Stranraer
Mull of Galloway
Workington
Annan
Solway Firth
Carlisle
ENGLAND
Consett
DURHAM
931 m ▲ Skiddaw
CUMBRIA
Penrith
Cross Fell ▲ 893 m
Tees
Eden

Land Height

Measured above Sea Level

- More than 1000 metres
- 500 – 1000 metres
- 200 – 500 metres
- 100 – 200 metres
- Less than 100 metres

Atlantic Ocean

18

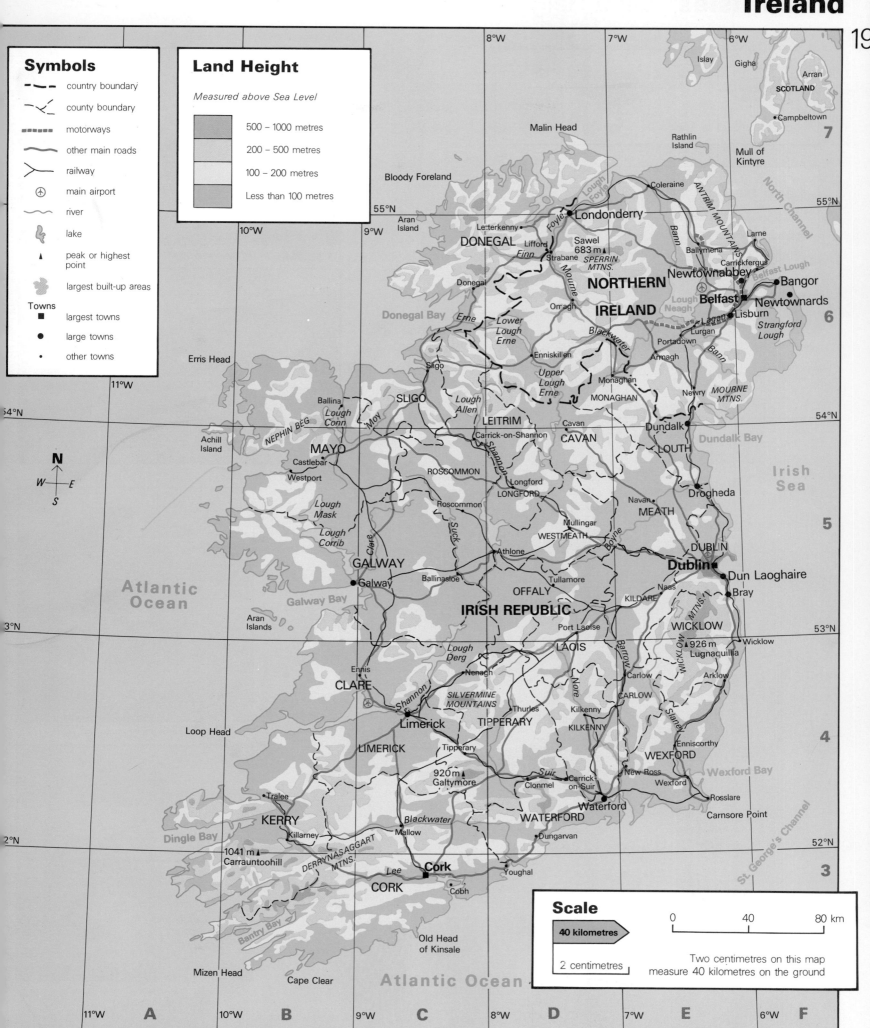

Symbols

- – – – country boundary
- ⌐–⌐ county boundary
- ▪▪▪▪▪▪ motorways
- ∼ other main roads
- ⤛ railway
- ✈ main airport
- ∼ river
- ▮ lake
- ▲ peak or highest point
- ▦ largest built-up areas

Towns
- ▪ largest towns
- ● large towns
- • other towns

Land Height

Measured above Sea Level

- 500 – 1000 metres
- 200 – 500 metres
- 100 – 200 metres
- Less than 100 metres

Scale

40 kilometres ▶

2 centimetres

0   40   80 km

Two centimetres on this map measure 40 kilometres on the ground

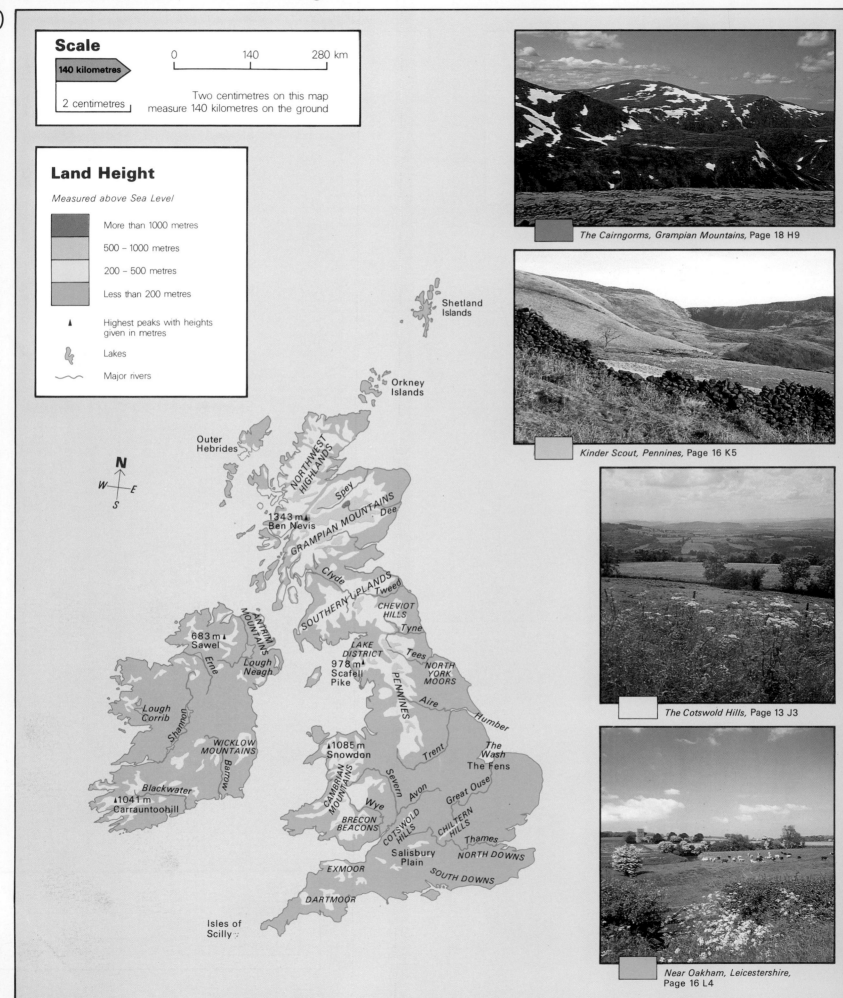

Scale

140 kilometres

2 centimetres

0   140   280 km

Two centimetres on this map
measure 140 kilometres on the ground

Land Height

Measured above Sea Level

More than 1000 metres

500 – 1000 metres

200 – 500 metres

Less than 200 metres

▲ Highest peaks with heights given in metres

Lakes

Major rivers

The Cairngorms, Grampian Mountains, Page 18 H9

Kinder Scout, Pennines, Page 16 K5

The Cotswold Hills, Page 13 J3

Near Oakham, Leicestershire, Page 16 L4

Shetland Islands

Orkney Islands

Outer Hebrides

N
W E
S

NORTHWEST HIGHLANDS

Spey

GRAMPIAN MOUNTAINS

Dee

1343 m ▲
Ben Nevis

Clyde

SOUTHERN UPLANDS

Tweed

CHEVIOT HILLS

Tyne

ANTRIM MOUNTAINS

683 m ▲
Sawel

Erne

Lough Neagh

LAKE DISTRICT
978 m ▲
Scafell Pike

Tees

NORTH YORK MOORS

PENNINES

Aire

Humber

Lough Corrib

Shannon

WICKLOW MOUNTAINS

Barrow

Blackwater

▲1041 m
Carrauntoohill

▲1085 m
Snowdon

CAMBRIAN MOUNTAINS

Severn

Wye

BRECON BEACONS

Avon

Trent

The Wash

The Fens

Great Ouse

COTSWOLD HILLS

CHILTERN HILLS

Thames

Salisbury Plain

NORTH DOWNS

SOUTH DOWNS

EXMOOR

DARTMOOR

Isles of Scilly

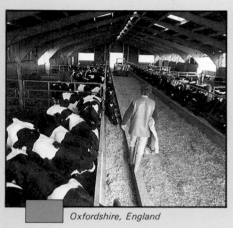

Oxfordshire, England

Oxfordshire, England

Scale

140 kilometres

2 centimetres

0   140   280 km

Two centimetres on this map measure 140 kilometres on the ground

Farms

Mostly livestock farms: farms where cattle or sheep are kept.

Mostly dairy farms: farms where cows are kept for milk.

Mostly arable farms: farms where crops are grown.

Mostly crofts: small farms where farmers grow crops and keep animals for their own use. On other farms crops and animals are sold.

Many farms in Britain are mixed farms. Farmers grow crops *and* keep animals.

🌲 **Forestry:** large areas where trees are grown for wood.

Sussex, England

Western Isles, Scotland

Highland Region, Scotland

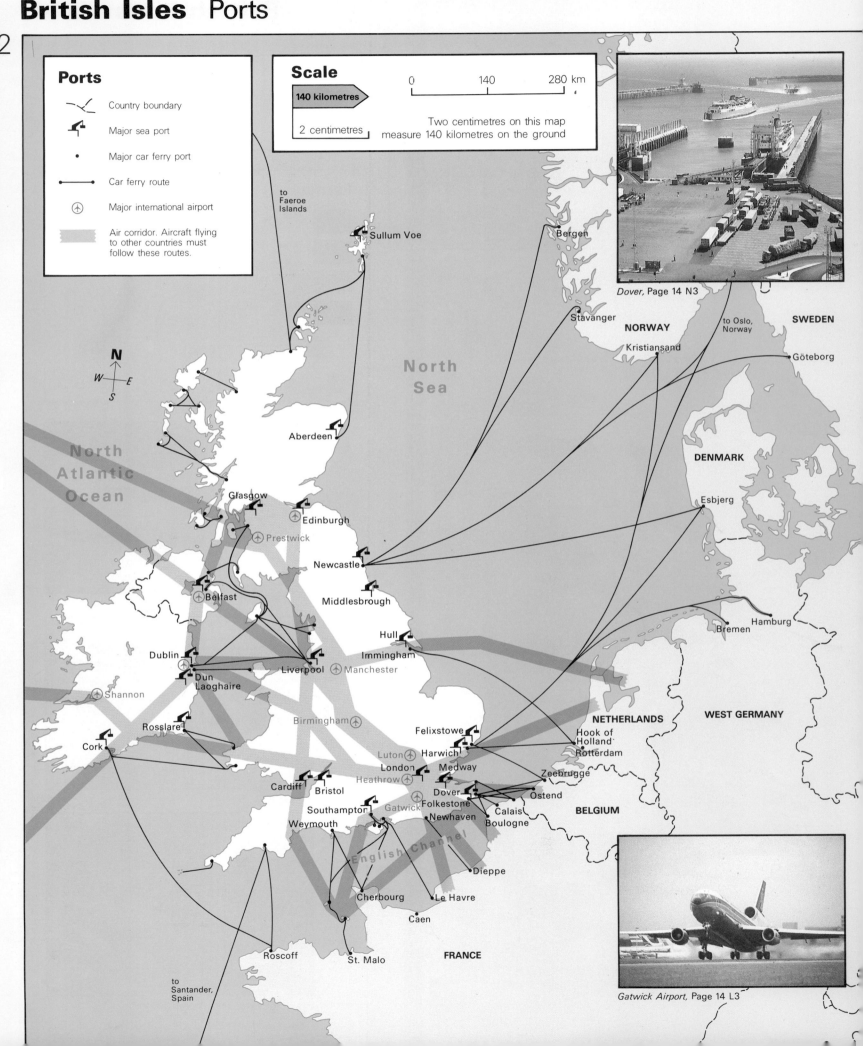

Ports

- ⌐ Country boundary
- ⚓ Major sea port
- • Major car ferry port
- •—• Car ferry route
- ✈ Major international airport
- Air corridor. Aircraft flying to other countries must follow these routes.

Scale

140 kilometres

2 centimetres

0   140   280 km

Two centimetres on this map measure 140 kilometres on the ground

Dover, Page 14 N3

to Faeroe Islands

Sullum Voe

Bergen

Stavanger

NORWAY

Kristiansand

to Oslo, Norway

SWEDEN

Göteborg

North Sea

DENMARK

Esbjerg

N
W   E
S

North Atlantic Ocean

Aberdeen

Glasgow

Edinburgh

Prestwick

Newcastle

Belfast

Middlesbrough

Hull

Immingham

Hamburg

Bremen

Dublin

Dun Laoghaire

Liverpool

Manchester

Shannon

Birmingham

NETHERLANDS

WEST GERMANY

Rosslare

Felixstowe

Harwich

Hook of Holland

Rotterdam

Cork

Luton

London

Medway

Zeebrugge

Cardiff

Bristol

Heathrow

Dover

Ostend

BELGIUM

Southampton

Gatwick

Folkestone

Newhaven

Calais

Weymouth

Boulogne

English Channel

Dieppe

Cherbourg

Le Havre

Caen

Roscoff

St. Malo

FRANCE

to Santander, Spain

Gatwick Airport, Page 14 L3

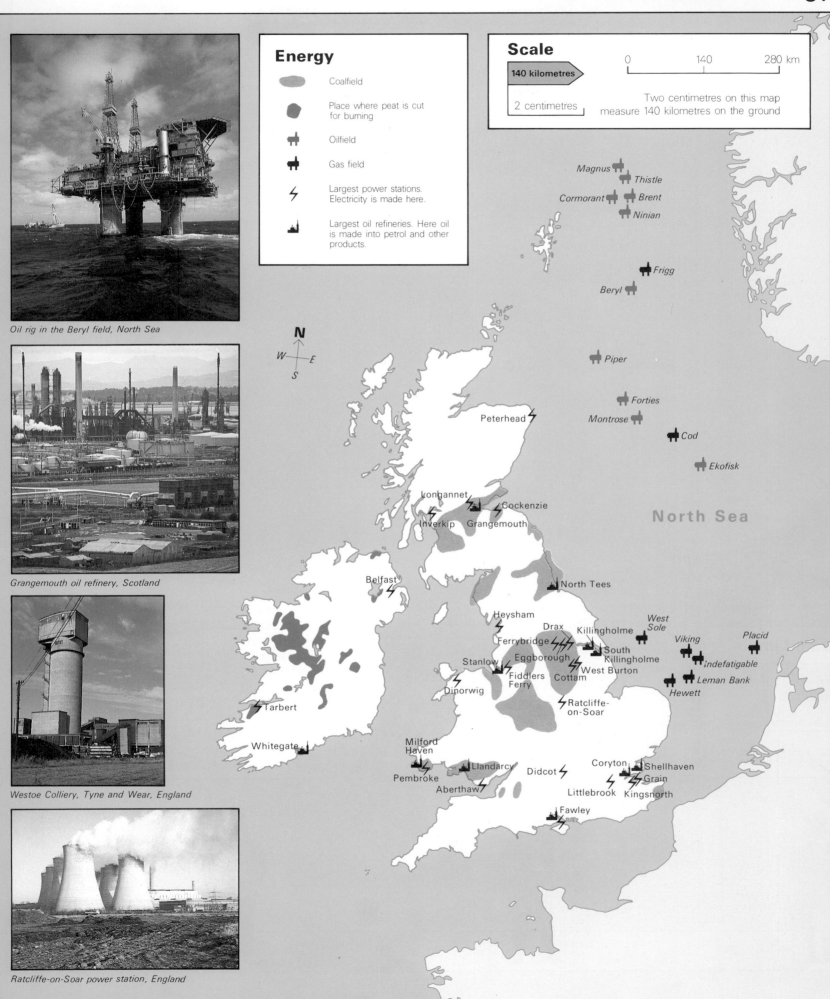

Energy

- ⬭ Coalfield
- ⬤ Place where peat is cut for burning
- ⛏ Oilfield
- ⛏ Gas field
- ⚡ Largest power stations. Electricity is made here.
- 🏭 Largest oil refineries. Here oil is made into petrol and other products.

Scale

140 kilometres

2 centimetres

0   140   280 km

Two centimetres on this map measure 140 kilometres on the ground

Oil rig in the Beryl field, North Sea

Grangemouth oil refinery, Scotland

Westoe Colliery, Tyne and Wear, England

Ratcliffe-on-Soar power station, England

Magnus
Thistle
Cormorant
Brent
Ninian

Frigg
Beryl

Piper

Forties
Montrose
Cod
Ekofisk

North Sea

Peterhead

Longannet
Cockenzie
Inverkip
Grangemouth

Belfast
North Tees

Heysham
Drax
West Sole
Killingholme
Viking
Placid
Ferrybridge
South Killingholme
Indefatigable
Stanlow
Eggborough
West Burton
Leman Bank
Fiddlers Ferry
Cottam
Hewett
Dinorwig
Ratcliffe-on-Soar

Tarbert

Whitegate

Milford Haven
Llandarcy
Didcot
Coryton
Shellhaven
Pembroke
Grain
Aberthaw
Littlebrook
Kingsnorth
Fawley

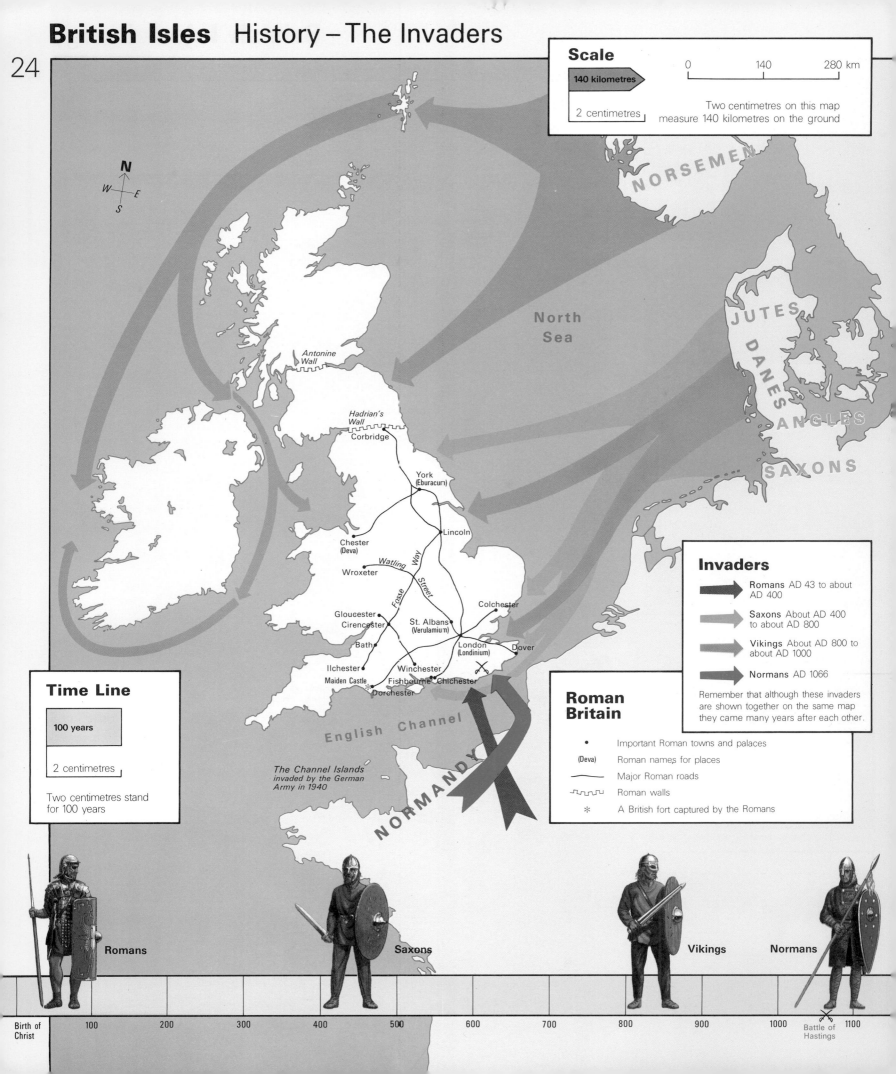

Scale

140 kilometres

2 centimetres

0   140   280 km

Two centimetres on this map measure 140 kilometres on the ground

NORSEMEN

North Sea

JUTES

DANES

ANGLES

SAXONS

Antonine Wall

Hadrian's Wall

Corbridge

York (Eburacum)

Lincoln

Chester (Deva)

Watling Street

Wroxeter

Fosse Street

Gloucester

Cirencester

St. Albans (Verulamium)

Colchester

Bath

London (Londinium)

Dover

Ilchester

Winchester

Maiden Castle

Fishbourne   Chichester

Dorchester

English Channel

The Channel Islands invaded by the German Army in 1940

NORMANDY

Invaders

Romans AD 43 to about AD 400

Saxons About AD 400 to about AD 800

Vikings About AD 800 to about AD 1000

Normans AD 1066

Remember that although these invaders are shown together on the same map they came many years after each other.

Roman Britain

•   Important Roman towns and palaces

(Deva)   Roman names for places

——   Major Roman roads

⊓⊔⊓⊔   Roman walls

*   A British fort captured by the Romans

Time Line

100 years

2 centimetres

Two centimetres stand for 100 years

Romans

Saxons

Vikings

Normans

Birth of Christ   100   200   300   400   500   600   700   800   900   1000   Battle of Hastings   1100

British Isles History—Battles and Castles

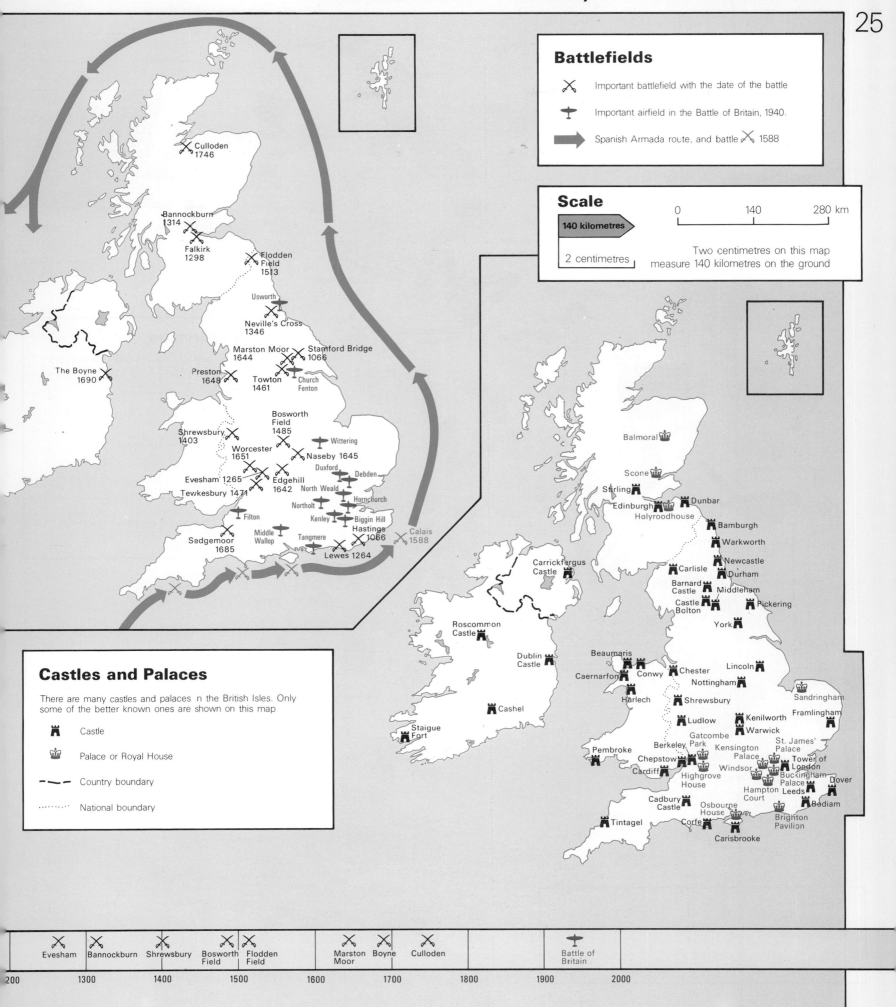

Battlefields

⚔ Important battlefield with the date of the battle

✈ Important airfield in the Battle of Britain, 1940.

➡ Spanish Armada route, and battle ⚔ 1588

Scale

140 kilometres	0	140	280 km
2 centimetres		Two centimetres on this map measure 140 kilometres on the ground	

Culloden 1746
Bannockburn 1314
Falkirk 1298
Flodden Field 1513
Usworth
Neville's Cross 1346
The Boyne 1690
Marston Moor 1644
Stamford Bridge 1066
Preston 1648
Towton 1461
Church Fenton
Bosworth Field 1485
Shrewsbury 1403
Wittering
Worcester 1651
Naseby 1645
Duxford
Debden
Evesham 1265
Edgehill 1642
North Weald
Tewkesbury 1471
Hornchurch
Northolt
Filton
Kenley
Biggin Hill
Middle Wallop
Hastings 1066
Sedgemoor 1685
Tangmere
Lewes 1264
Calais 1588

Castles and Palaces

There are many castles and palaces in the British Isles. Only some of the better known ones are shown on this map

🏰 Castle

♛ Palace or Royal House

– – – Country boundary

········· National boundary

Balmoral
Scone
Stirling
Edinburgh
Holyroodhouse
Dunbar
Bamburgh
Warkworth
Carrickfergus Castle
Carlisle
Newcastle
Durham
Barnard Castle
Middleham
Castle Bolton
Pickering
York
Roscommon Castle
Beaumaris
Chester
Lincoln
Dublin Castle
Caernarfon
Conwy
Nottingham
Harlech
Shrewsbury
Sandringham
Cashel
Ludlow
Kenilworth
Framlingham
Warwick
Staigue Fort
Berkeley
Gatcombe Park
Kensington Palace
St. James' Palace
Pembroke
Chepstow
Windsor
Tower of London
Cardiff
Highgrove House
Buckingham Palace
Hampton Court
Leeds
Bediam
Cadbury Castle
Osbourne House
Dover
Tintagel
Corfe
Carisbrooke
Brighton Pavilion

⚔	⚔	⚔	⚔	⚔		⚔	⚔	⚔		✈
Evesham	Bannockburn	Shrewsbury	Bosworth Field	Flodden Field		Marston Moor	Boyne	Culloden		Battle of Britain
200	1300	1400	1500	1600		1700	1800	1900	2000	

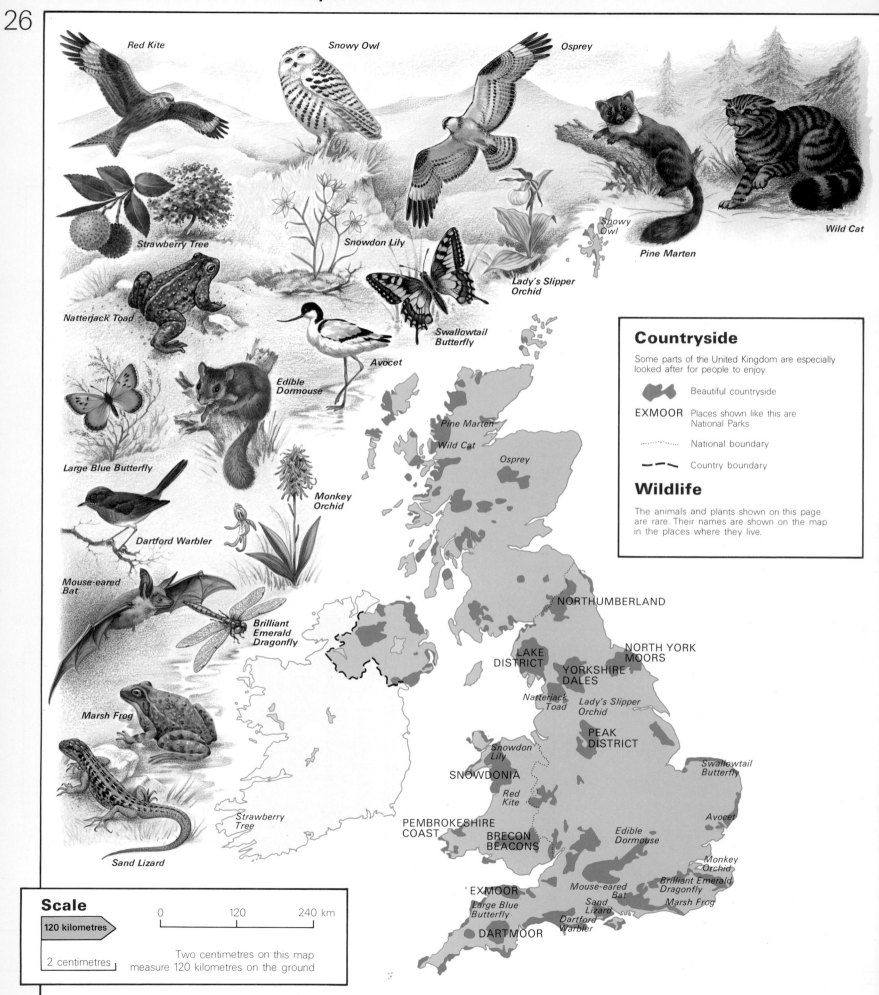

Red Kite

Snowy Owl

Osprey

Wild Cat

Strawberry Tree

Snowdon Lily

Snowy Owl

Pine Marten

Lady's Slipper Orchid

Natterjack Toad

Swallowtail Butterfly

Avocet

Edible Dormouse

Large Blue Butterfly

Monkey Orchid

Dartford Warbler

Mouse-eared Bat

Brilliant Emerald Dragonfly

Marsh Frog

Sand Lizard

Countryside

Some parts of the United Kingdom are especially looked after for people to enjoy.

Beautiful countryside

EXMOOR Places shown like this are National Parks

.... National boundary

— — — Country boundary

Wildlife

The animals and plants shown on this page are rare. Their names are shown on the map in the places where they live.

Pine Marten

Wild Cat

Osprey

NORTHUMBERLAND

NORTH YORK MOORS

LAKE DISTRICT

YORKSHIRE DALES

Natterjack Toad

Lady's Slipper Orchid

PEAK DISTRICT

Snowdon Lily

Swallowtail Butterfly

SNOWDONIA

Red Kite

Avocet

PEMBROKESHIRE COAST

Edible Dormouse

BRECON BEACONS

Monkey Orchid

Brilliant Emerald Dragonfly

Strawberry Tree

EXMOOR

Mouse-eared Bat

Large Blue Butterfly

Sand Lizard

Marsh Frog

Dartford Warbler

DARTMOOR

Scale

120 kilometres

0   120   240 km

2 centimetres

Two centimetres on this map measure 120 kilometres on the ground

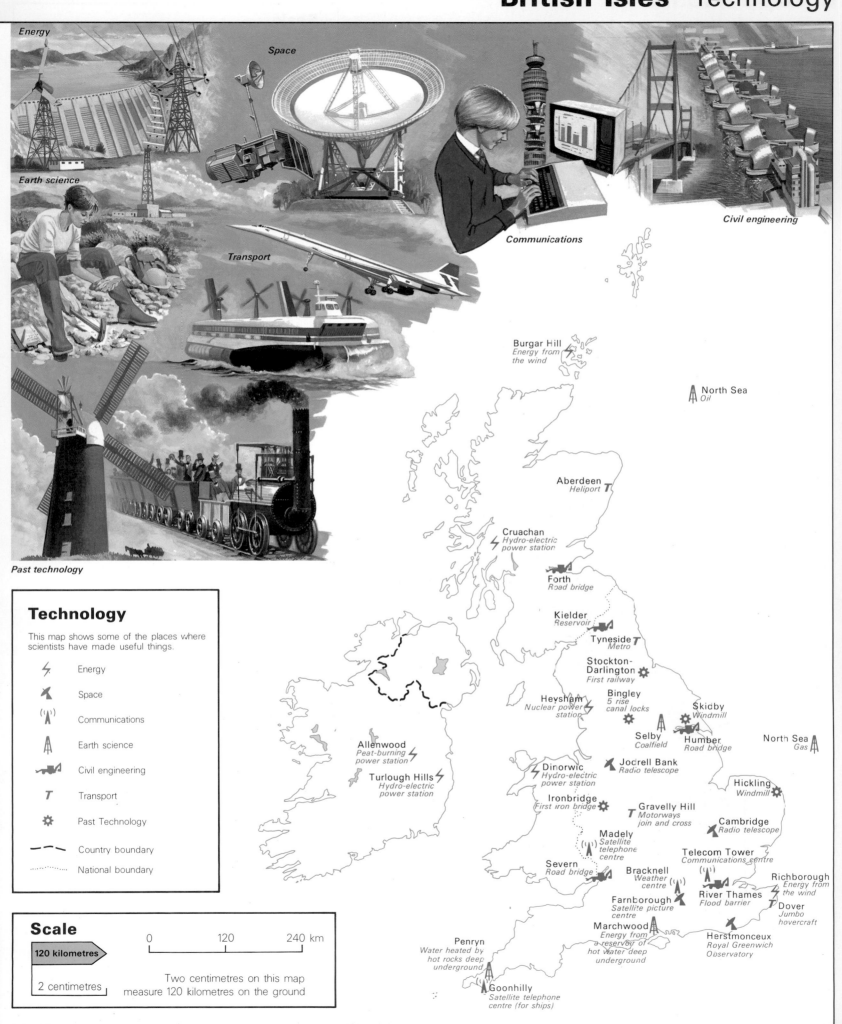

Energy

Space

Earth science

Transport

Communications

Civil engineering

Past technology

Technology

This map shows some of the places where scientists have made useful things.

⚡	Energy
🛰	Space
(ᵗᵢᵗ)	Communications
🗼	Earth science
🚜	Civil engineering
T	Transport
✺	Past Technology
— — —	Country boundary
·········	National boundary

Scale

120 kilometres

2 centimetres

0   120   240 km

Two centimetres on this map
measure 120 kilometres on the ground

Burgar Hill
*Energy from
the wind*

North Sea
Oil

Aberdeen
Heliport T

Cruachan
*Hydro-electric
power station*

Forth
Road bridge

Kielder
Reservoir

Tyneside
Metro T

Stockton-
Darlington
First railway

Bingley
*5 rise
canal locks*

Skidby
Windmill

Heysham
*Nuclear power
station*

Selby
Coalfield

Humber
Road bridge

North Sea
Gas

Allenwood
*Peat-burning
power station*

Dinorwic
*Hydro-electric
power station*

Jodrell Bank
Radio telescope

Turlough Hills
*Hydro-electric
power station*

Ironbridge
First iron bridge

Gravelly Hill
*Motorways
join and cross* T

Hickling
Windmill

Cambridge
Radio telescope

Madely
*Satellite
telephone
centre*

Telecom Tower
Communications centre

Severn
Road bridge

Bracknell
*Weather
centre*

Richborough
*Energy from
the wind*

River Thames
Flood barrier

Dover
*Jumbo
hovercraft* T

Farnborough
*Satellite picture
centre*

Penryn
*Water heated by
hot rocks deep
underground*

Marchwood
*Energy from
a reservoir of
hot water deep
underground*

Herstmonceux
*Royal Greenwich
Observatory*

Goonhilly
*Satellite telephone
centre (for ships)*

Europe Countries

28

NORTH

Arctic
Ocean

Scale

400 kilometres

2 centimetres

0   400   800 km

Two centimetres on this map
measure 400 kilometres on the ground

Reykjavik ★ **ICELAND**

Arctic Circle

Murmansk

Narvik

N O R W A Y

Trondheim

FINLAND

Faeroe
Islands
(Denmark)

Shetland
Islands
(U.K.)

Bergen

S W E D E N

Orkney
Islands
(U.K.)

Oslo

Helsinki

Leningrad

North
Atlantic
Ocean

Stavanger

Stockholm

Gor'kiy

Kazan

Glasgow

North Sea

Göteborg

Belfast

Riga

Moscow

**IRISH
REPUBLIC**

Dublin

**UNITED
KINGDOM**

DENMARK

Copenhagen

Malmo

Baltic Sea

Kaliningrad

Minsk

Cork

Birmingham

NETHERLANDS

Hamburg

Gdańsk

Cardiff

Amsterdam

**West
Berlin**

East Berlin

P O L A N D

UNION OF SOVIET SOCIALIST REPUBLICS

London

Rotterdam

Channel
Islands
(U.K.)

Cherbourg

Brussels

BELGIUM

Bonn

EAST
GERMANY

Warsaw

Kiev

Kharkov

LUXEMBOURG

Prague

Paris

WEST
GERMANY

CZECHOSLOVAKIA

Dnepropetrovsk

Donetsk

Nantes

F R A N C E

Munich

Vienna

Bay of
Biscay

Bern

AUSTRIA

Budapest

R O M A N I A

Odessa

Bordeaux

SWITZERLAND

LIECHTENSTEIN

HUNGARY

Lyons

Milan

Trieste

Sevastopol

Bilbao

Turin

Black Sea

Oporto

Belgrade

Bucharest

Constanta

ANDORRA

Marseille

MONACO

SAN
MARINO

YUGOSLAVIA

BULGARIA

Lisbon

Madrid

Barcelona

Corsica
(France)

I
T
A
L
Y

Adriatic Sea

Sofiya

Istanbul

PORTUGAL

S P A I N

Rome

Tiranë

Thessalonica

Ankara

Seville

Sardinia
(Italy)

Naples

ALBANIA

T U R K E Y

Gibraltar
(U.K.)

Balearic Islands
(Spain)

GREECE

Aegean Sea

Palermo

Sicily
(Italy)

Nicosia

Symbols

Rome   Cities with this type of lettering
             have more than 1 million people

★   Capital cities

•   Other cities

ITALY   The names of countries are shown
             with this type of lettering

⌄   Country boundary

—   Main roads

⋈   Main railways

MALTA

Athens

CYPRUS

Crete
(Greece)

Mediterranean Sea

SOUTH

Scale

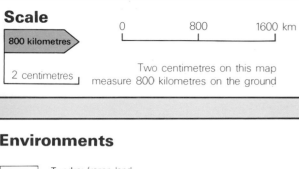

800 kilometres

2 centimetres

0   800   1600 km

Two centimetres on this map
measure 800 kilometres on the ground

Environments

Tundra: frozen land.

Cold forests: mostly coniferous trees.

Deserts: sand, stones, short grass or shrubs.

Mountains: high peaks and valleys.

Marsh: land under water.

Farmland: land used for growing crops.

Grazing land: land used for keeping animals.

▲ Highest peaks with heights given in metres

Lakes

Largest rivers

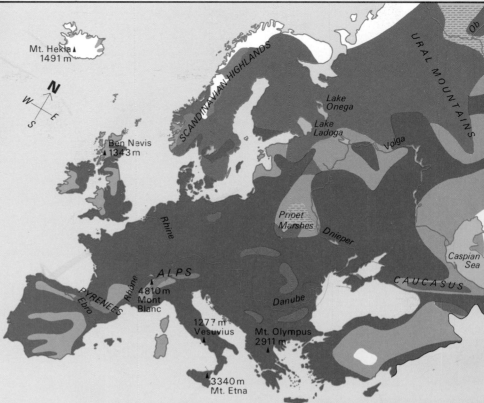

Mt. Hekla
1491 m

SCANDINAVIAN HIGHLANDS

URAL MOUNTAINS

Lake Onega

Lake Ladoga

Ob

Volga

Ben Nevis
1343 m

Rhine

Pripet Marshes

Dnieper

Caspian Sea

ALPS

Rhône

Ebro

PYRENEES

4810 m
Mont Blanc

Danube

CAUCASUS

1277 m
Vesuvius

Mt. Olympus
2911 m

3340 m
Mt. Etna

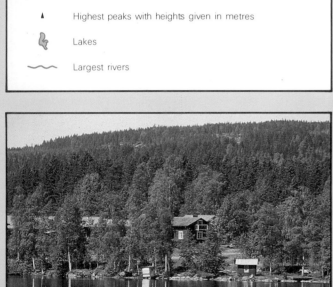

Sweden

Italy

Czechoslovakia

France

France

Scale

	0	400	800 km

400 kilometres

2 centimetres

Two centimetres on this map measure 400 kilometres on the ground

Symbols

Symbol	Description
☀	Seaside holidays
⩕	Mountain and winter sports holidays
⛵	Sailing holidays and cruises
•	Sightseeing holidays
Paris	This type of lettering shows capital cities
Majorca	This type of lettering shows major holiday areas
Lourdes	This type of lettering shows other holiday centres, famous buildings, museums or events.
⌇	Country boundary

Reykjavik
Hot springs and glaciers

Norwegian Fiords

Scottish Highlands

Oslo

Finnish Lake District

Helsinki

Stockholm

• Edinburgh

Lake District

Dublin

Blarney Stone

Baltic Sea

Legoland

Copenhagen
Little Mermaid

Moscow •
Red Square

Stratford

Amsterdam
Dutch bulb fields

London

English Channel

Channel Islands

Brussels

Berlin

Warsaw

• **Bonn**

Luxembourg

• **Paris**
Eiffel tower
Versailles

Brittany

Chateaux of the River Loire

Black Forest

Bavaria

• **Prague**

Oberammergau

Salzburg

Bern

• **Vienna**

Budapest

A l p s

Venice

Belgrade

Bucharest

Black Sea

Lourdes

Pyrenees

Monte Carlo

Riviera

Côte d'Azur

Florence

Pisa

Limestone Caves

Sofiya

Adriatic Sea

Lisbon

• **Madrid**

Costa Brava

Minorca

Rome
Vatican

Mt. Vesuvius

Tiranë

Istanbul

• **Ankara**

Algarve

Granada

Costa Blanca

Ibiza

Majorca

Corfu

Ionian Sea

Greek Islands

Aegean Sea

Costa del Sol

Athens
Acropolis

Crete

Malta

Mediterranean Sea

N
W E
S

Majorca, Spain

Scale

300 kilometres

2 centimetres

0   300   600 km

Two centimetres on this map
measure 300 kilometres on the ground

Car factory, Turin, Italy

European Community

The European Community is also known
as the *EEC* (which stands for European
Economic Community) or the *Common
Market*. It is a group of countries which
have agreed to work together and to
share the same plans for industry,
agriculture, transport and trade.

Countries which are members of
the European Community.

These countries join the
European Community in 1986.

Country boundary.

FRANCE The names of countries are shown
with this type of lettering.

Factories

Industrial areas. Places with
many factories.

Ruhr Major industrial areas are shown
with this type of lettering.

Cars

Ships

Clothes

Machines (factories that make
machines for other factories).

Electrical goods (for example,
computers, televisions, fridges
and washing machines).

Oil refineries (turning oil into
other products such as petrol).

Iron and steel (to be used by
other factories).

Glasgow
Grangemouth
**UNITED
KINGDOM**
**IRISH
REPUBLIC**
*Northern
England*
Manchester
Stanlow
Midlands
Pembroke/
Milford Haven
London
Fawley
DENMARK
Copenhagen
Hamburg
NETHERLANDS
Bremen
Eindhoven
Rotterdam
Hanover
Berlin
Antwerp
Wolfsburg
Lille
BELGIUM
Ruhr
**WEST
GERMANY**
Charleroi
Liège
Le Havre
Frankfurt
LUXEMBOURG
Paris
Metz
Nuremburg
Saarbrucken
FRANCE
Stuttgart
Munich
Lyons
Milan
*River
Rhône*
River Po
Turin
Marseille
Ravenna
PORTUGAL
SPAIN
ITALY
Barcelona
Naples
Algeciras
Taranto
Cagliari
GREECE
Athens
Messina
Ragusa

Asia Countries

British Isles

Scale

800 kilometres

2 centimetres

0   800   1600 km

Two centimetres on this map measure 800 kilometres on the ground

Arctic Ocean

Baltic Sea

St. Lawren. (U.S.A.)

Leningrad

Arkhangel'sk

Vorkuta

Magadan

Minsk

Arctic Circle

Moscow

Gor'kiy

UNION OF SOVIET SOCIALIST REPUBLICS

Yakutsk

Sea of Okhotsk

Kiev

Perm

Odessa

Kharkóv

Sverdlovsk

Kuril Islan (U.S.S

Dnepropetrovsk

Donetsk

Kuybyshev

Istanbul

Sevastopol

Chelyabinsk

Omsk

Novosibirsk

Chita

Sapporo

Black Sea

Astrakhan'

Lake Baykal

Ankara

Irkutsk

Ulan-Ude

Harbin

Vladivostok

TURKEY

Gur'yev

Tbilisi

Caspian Sea

Ulan Bator

Changchun

JAPAN

Yerevan

Aral Sea

Lake Balkhash

MONGOLIA

Shenyang

Fushun

NORTH KOREA

SYRIA

Baku

Tashkent

Anshan

Tokyo

IRAQ

Mashhad

Wulumuchi

Peking

Tientsin

Lüta

Pyongyang

Seoul

SOUTH KOREA

Nagoya

Baghdad

Tehran

IRAN

Taiyuan

Tsingtao

Tsinan

Pusan

Osaka

Basra

KUWAIT

Kabul

Lanchow

Sian

Yellow Sea

Kitakyus

Kuwait

SAUDI

Bushire

AFGHANISTAN

Jammu and Kashmir

Chengchow

Ryukyu Islands (Japan)

BAHRAIN

Riyadh

QATAR

Doha

Islamabad

CHINA

Nanking

Shanghai

ARABIA

UNITED ARAB EMIRATES

Lahore

PAKISTAN

NEPAL

Chengtu

Wuhan

Muscat

Delhi

Katmandu

Thimpu

Chungking

Taipei

OMAN

Karachi

Kanpur

BHUTAN

TAIWAN

Kaohsiung

SOUTH YEMEN

Ahmadabad

BANGLADESH

Kunming

Canton

Hong Kong (U.K.)

Macao (Portugal)

Nagpur

Dacca

Socotra (South Yemen)

Arabian Sea

Bombay

INDIA

Calcutta

BURMA

Hanoi

Haiphong

Pune

Hyderabad

Vientiane

VIETNAM

Manila

Rangoon

THAILAND

South China Sea

PHILIPPINES

Bangalore

Madras

Bay of Bengal

Bangkok

KAMPUCHEA

Andaman Islands (India)

Phnom Penh

Ho Chi Minh City (Saigon)

Symbols

Omsk   Cities with this type of lettering have more than 1 million people

★   Capital cities

•   Other cities

JAPAN   The names of countries are shown with this type of lettering

⌐⌐   Country boundary

——   Main roads

〰   Main railways

SRI LANKA

Colombo

Nicobar Islands (India)

BRUNEI

Bandar Seri Begawan

Banda Acheh

MALAYSIA

Kuala Lumpur

N

W   E

S

SINGAPORE

Equator

INDONESIA

Palembang

Java Sea

Jakarta

Bandung

Surabaya

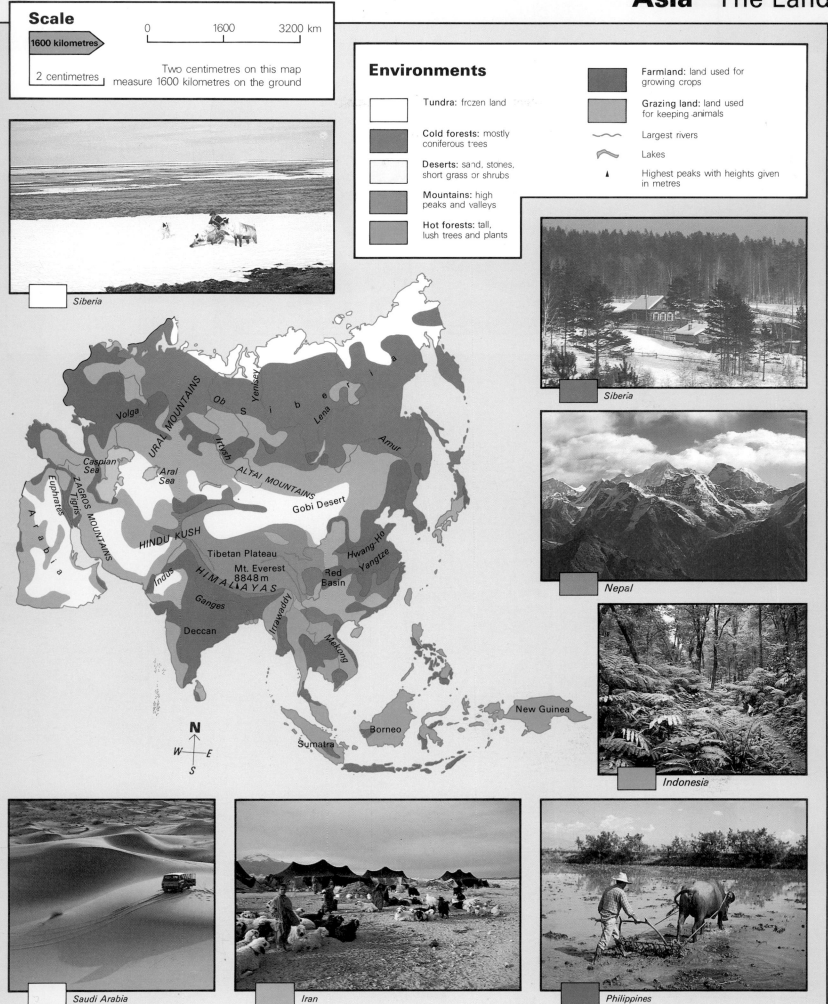

Scale

1600 kilometres

2 centimetres

0   1600   3200 km

Two centimetres on this map
measure 1600 kilometres on the ground

Environments

Tundra: frozen land

Cold forests: mostly
coniferous trees

Deserts: sand, stones,
short grass or shrubs

Mountains: high
peaks and valleys

Hot forests: tall,
lush trees and plants

Farmland: land used for
growing crops

Grazing land: land used
for keeping animals

Largest rivers

Lakes

Highest peaks with heights given
in metres

Siberia

Siberia

Nepal

Indonesia

Saudi Arabia

Iran

Philippines

Map labels

Volga
URAL MOUNTAINS
Ob
Yenisey
S i b e r i a
Lena
Amur
Irtysh
ALTAI MOUNTAINS
Caspian Sea
Aral Sea
Gobi Desert
Euphrates
Tigris
ZAGROS MOUNTAINS
HINDU KUSH
Arabia
Tibetan Plateau
Mt. Everest 8848 m
Hwang-Ho
Yangtze
Red Basin
Indus
HIMALAYAS
Ganges
Deccan
Irrawaddy
Mekong
New Guinea
Borneo
Sumatra

N
W   E
S

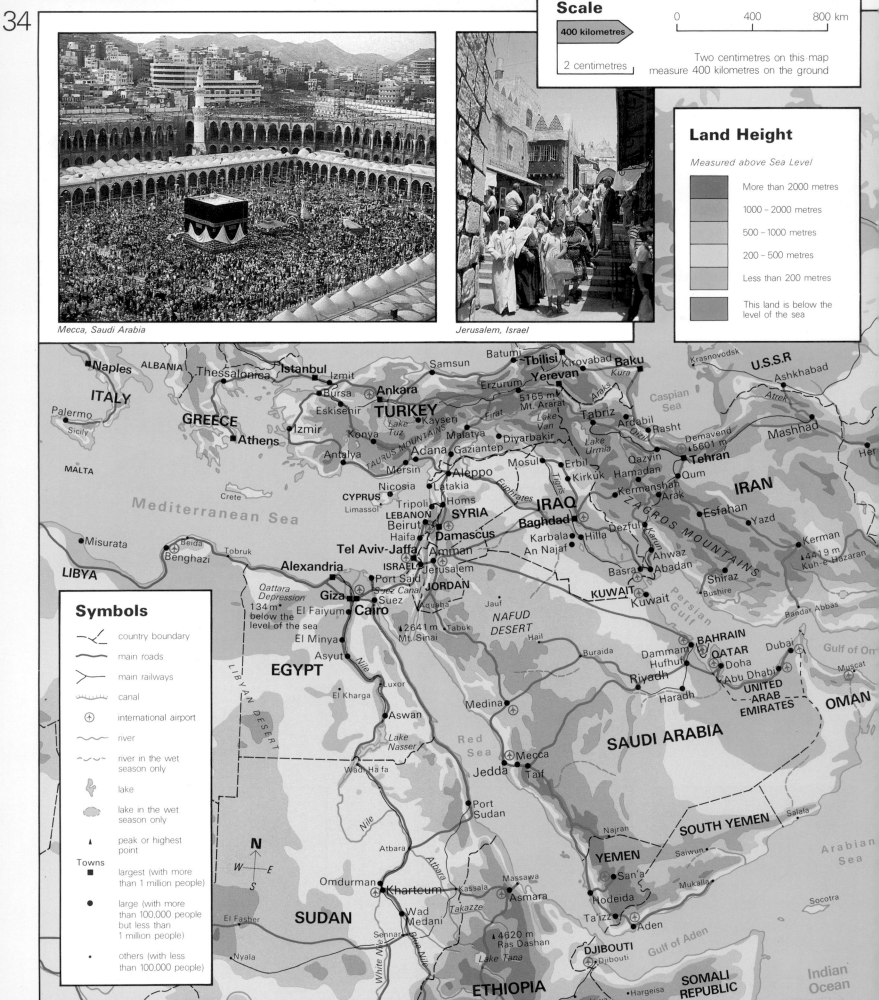

Mecca, Saudi Arabia

Jerusalem, Israel

Scale

| 0 | 400 | 800 km |

400 kilometres

2 centimetres

Two centimetres on this map
measure 400 kilometres on the ground

Land Height

Measured above Sea Level

More than 2000 metres

1000 – 2000 metres

500 – 1000 metres

200 – 500 metres

Less than 200 metres

This land is below the
level of the sea

Symbols

country boundary

main roads

main railways

canal

international airport

river

river in the wet
season only

lake

lake in the wet
season only

peak or highest
point

Towns

■ largest (with more
than 1 million people)

● large (with more
than 100,000 people
but less than
1 million people)

• others (with less
than 100,000 people)

Naples ALBANIA Thessalonica Istanbul Izmit Samsun Batumi Tbilisi Kirovabad Baku Krasnovodsk U.S.S.R.
ITALY GREECE Bursa Ankara Erzurum Yerevan Kura Ashkhabad
Palermo Eskisehir TURKEY 5165 m Mt. Ararat Araks Caspian Atrek
Sicily Athens Izmir Konya Kayseri Lake Malatya Lake Van Tabriz Ardabil Rasht Demavend Mashhad
MALTA Antalya TAURUS MOUNTAINS Adana Gaziantep Mosul Erbil Qazvin Hamadan Qum Tehran 5601 m
Mersin Aleppo Kirkuk Kermanshah IRAN Her
Crete Nicosia Latakia Euphrates Tigris Arak Esfahan Yazd
Mediterranean Sea CYPRUS Tripoli Homs SYRIA IRAQ Dezful Kerman
Limassol LEBANON Beirut Damascus Baghdad Karun Ahwaz 4419 m Kuh-e-Hazaran
Misurata Beida Haifa Tel Aviv-Jaffa Amman Karbala Hilla Basra Abadan Shiraz
Benghazi Tobruk ISRAEL Jerusalem An Najaf Bushire ZAGROS MOUNTAINS
LIBYA Alexandria Port Said JORDAN KUWAIT Bandar Abbas
Qattara Suez Canal Aqaba Jauf Kuwait Persian
Depression Giza Suez NAFUD Gulf of Om
134 m El Faiyum Cairo 2641 m DESERT Gulf
below the Mt. Sinai Tabuk Hail BAHRAIN Dubai
level of the sea El Minya Buraida Dammam QATAR Muscat
Asyut Hufhuf Doha OMAN
EGYPT LIBYAN DESERT Luxor Riyadh Abu Dhabi UNITED
El Kharga Medina Haradh ARAB
Aswan EMIRATES
Lake Red SAUDI ARABIA
Nasser Sea Mecca
Wadi Ha fa Jedda Taif
Nile Port SOUTH YEMEN Salala
Sudan Najran Saiwun Mukalla
N Atbara YEMEN Arabian
W E San'a Sea
S Massawa Hodeida Ta'izz
Omdurman Kharteum Kassala Asmara Ras Dashan Aden
El Fasher Wad Takazze DJIBOUTI Gulf of Aden Socotra
SUDAN Medani 4620 m Djibouti
Nyala Sennar Ras Dashan SOMALI Indian
White Nile Blue Nile Lake Tana REPUBLIC Ocean
Malakal ETHIOPIA Hargeisa
Diredawa

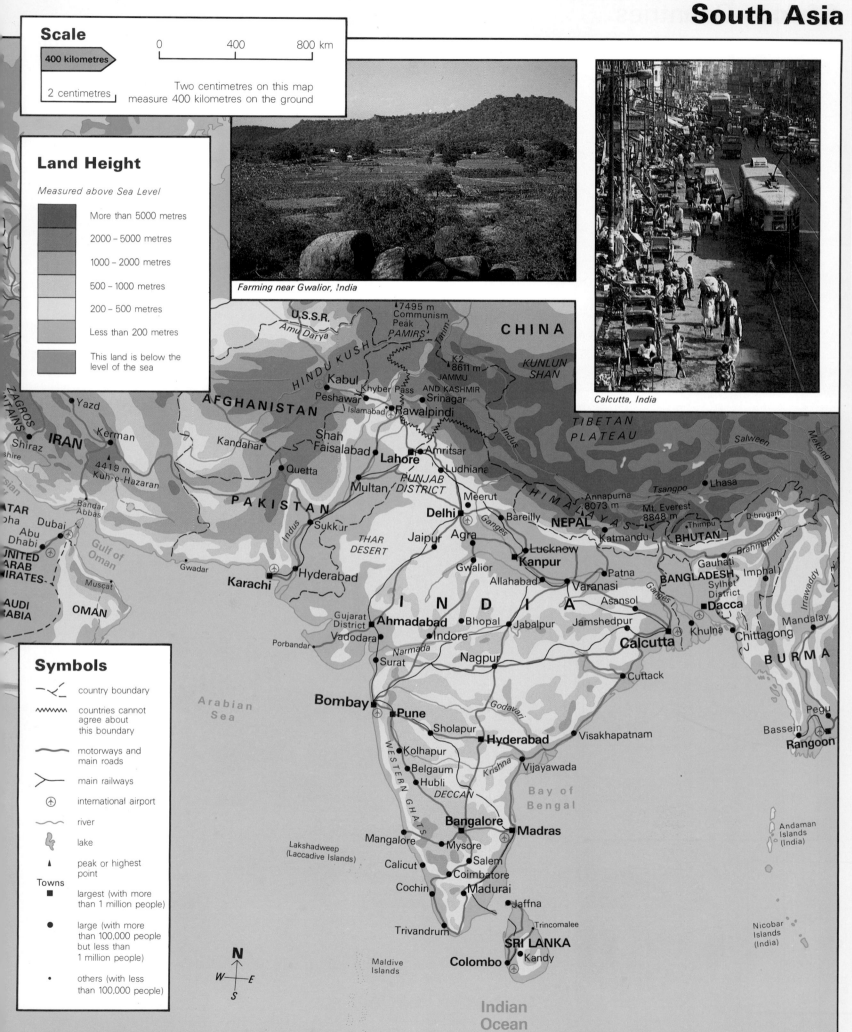

Scale

Land Height

Measured above Sea Level

More than 5000 metres

2000 – 5000 metres

1000 – 2000 metres

500 – 1000 metres

200 – 500 metres

Less than 200 metres

This land is below the
level of the sea

Farming near Gwalior, India

Calcutta, India

Symbols

country boundary

countries cannot
agree about
this boundary

motorways and
main roads

main railways

international airport

river

lake

peak or highest
point

Towns

largest (with more
than 1 million people)

large (with more
than 100,000 people
but less than
1 million people)

others (with less
than 100,000 people)

U.S.S.R.

Amu Darya

7495 m
Communism
Peak
PAMIRS

Tarim

CHINA

HINDU KUSH

Kabul

Khyber Pass

K2
8611 m

*KUNLUN
SHAN*

*TIBETAN
PLATEAU*

Salween

Mekong

ZAGROS
TAINS

Yazd

AFGHANISTAN

Peshawar
Islamabad
Rawalpindi

JAMMU
AND KASHMIR

Srinagar

IRAN

Kerman

Kandahar

Shah
Faisalabad

Amritsar

Lhasa

Shiraz
shire

4419 m
Kuh-e-Hazaran

Quetta

Lahore

Ludhiana

HIMALAYAS

Annapurna
8073 m

Tsangpo

PAKISTAN

Multan

*PUNJAB
DISTRICT*

Meerut

NEPAL

Katmandu

Mt. Everest
8848 m

Thimpu

Dibrugarh

TAR
oha
Dubai
Abu
Dhabi

Bandar
Abbas

Sukkur

Delhi

Bareilly

BHUTAN

Gauhati

Brahmaputra

Imphal

UNITED
ARAB
IRATES

Gulf of
Oman

Indus

*THAR
DESERT*

Jaipur

Agra

Lucknow

Kanpur

Patna

BANGLADESH

Sylhet
District

AUDI
ABIA

Muscat

Gwadar

Karachi

Hyderabad

Gwalior

Allahabad

Varanasi

Ganges

Asansol

Ganges

Dacca

Mandalay

OMAN

INDIA

Ahmadabad

Bhopal

Jabalpur

Jamshedpur

Khulna

Chittagong

Irrawaddy

Gujarat
District

Vadodara

Indore

Calcutta

BURMA

Porbandar

Narmada

Surat

Nagpur

Cuttack

Arabian
Sea

Bombay

Pune

Godavari

Pegu

Sholapur

Hyderabad

Visakhapatnam

Bassein

Kolhapur

Krishna

Vijayawada

Rangoon

Belgaum

Hubli

DECCAN

Bay of
Bengal

WESTERN GHATS

Bangalore

Madras

Andaman
Islands
(India)

Lakshadweep
(Laccadive Islands)

Mangalore

Mysore

Calicut

Salem

Coimbatore

Cochin

Madurai

Jaffna

Nicobar
Islands
(India)

Trincomalee

Trivandrum

SRI LANKA

N
W   E
S

Maldive
Islands

Colombo

Kandy

Indian
Ocean

Africa Countries

Scale

800 kilometres

2 centimetres

0   800   1600 km

Two centimetres on this map measure 800 kilometres on the ground

N
W   E
S

North Atlantic Ocean

Mediterranean Sea

Madeira (Portugal)

Tetuan
Algiers
Tunis
Rabat
Casablanca
Marrakesh
MOROCCO
TUNISIA
Tripoli
Alexandria
Cairo
Suez

Canary Islands (Spain)

ALGERIA
LIBYA
EGYPT

Red Sea

CAPE VERDE ISLANDS

MAURITANIA
Nouakchott
MALI
NIGER
CHAD
Khartoum
Port Sudan
Asmara

SUDAN

Dakar
SENEGAL
GAMBIA
Banjul
GUINEA-BISSAU
Bissau
GUINEA
Conakry
Freetown
SIERRA LEONE
Monrovia
LIBERIA
Bamako
BURKINA FASO
Ouagadougou
Niamey
Kano
NIGERIA
Abuja
N'Djamena
DJIBOUTI
Djibouti
Addis Ababa
ETHIOPIA

IVORY COAST
GHANA
TOGO
BENIN
Ibadan
Lagos
Abidjan
Accra
Lomé
Porto Novo
Port Harcourt
CAMEROUN
Douala
Yaoundé
Bangui
CENTRAL AFRICAN REPUBLIC
SOMALI REPUBLIC
Mogadiscio

Equator

Gulf of Guinea
EQUATORIAL GUINEA
Malabo
PRINCIPE
SÃO TOMÉ
Libreville
GABON
CONGO
Brazzaville
Pointe Noire
Kinshasa
Matadi
ZAÏRE
Kananga
UGANDA
Kampala
KENYA
Nairobi
Mombasa
RWANDA
Kigali
BURUNDI
Bujumbura
TANZANIA
Dodoma
Dar es Salaam

Indian Ocean

Luanda
ANGOLA
Benguela

COMORO ISLANDS

MALAWI
Lilongwe
Blantyre
Mahajanga
Mozambique

South Atlantic Ocean

ZAMBIA
Lusaka
MOZAMBIQUE
Beira
Antananarivo
Toamasina
MADAGASCAR
Réunion (France)

Harare
ZIMBABWE
NAMIBIA
Walvis Bay
Windhoek
BOTSWANA
Gaborone
Pretoria
Johannesburg
Maputo
SWAZILAND
Mbabane
Toliara

SOUTH AFRICA
LESOTHO
Maseru
Durban
East London
Port Elizabeth
Cape Town

Symbols

Cairo   Cities with this type of lettering have more than 1 million people

★   Capital cities

•   Other cities

MALI   The names of countries are shown with this type of lettering

〰   Country boundary

〰   Main roads

〰   Main railways

This is the size of the British Isles compared with Africa

Scale

1200 kilometres

2 centimetres

0   1200   2400 km

Two centimetres on this map
measure 1200 kilometres on the ground

Environments

Desert: sand stones, short grass or shrubs.

Mountains: high peaks and valleys.

Marsh: land under water.

Hot forest: tall, lush trees and plants.

Savanna: tall, thick grasses.

Farmland: land used for growing crops.

Grazing land: land used for keeping animals.

▲ Highest peaks with heights given in metres

Lakes

Largest rivers

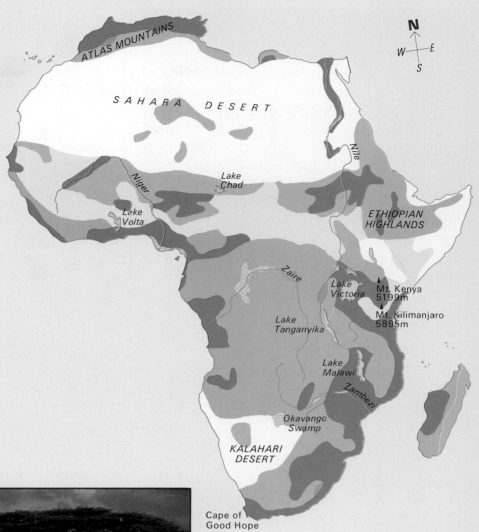

ATLAS MOUNTAINS

SAHARA DESERT

Nile

Niger

Lake Chad

Leke Volta

ETHIOPIAN HIGHLANDS

Zaïre

Lake Victoria

Mt. Kenya 5199m

Mt. Kilimanjaro 5895m

Lake Tanganyika

Lake Malawi

Zambezi

Okavango Swamp

KALAHARI DESERT

Cape of Good Hope

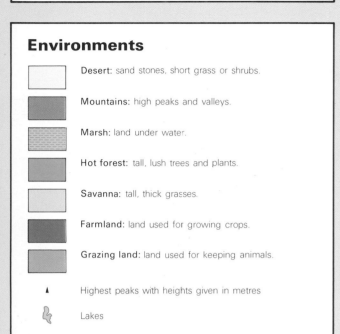

Niger

Kenya

Nigeria

Botswana

Nigeria

Australasia Countries

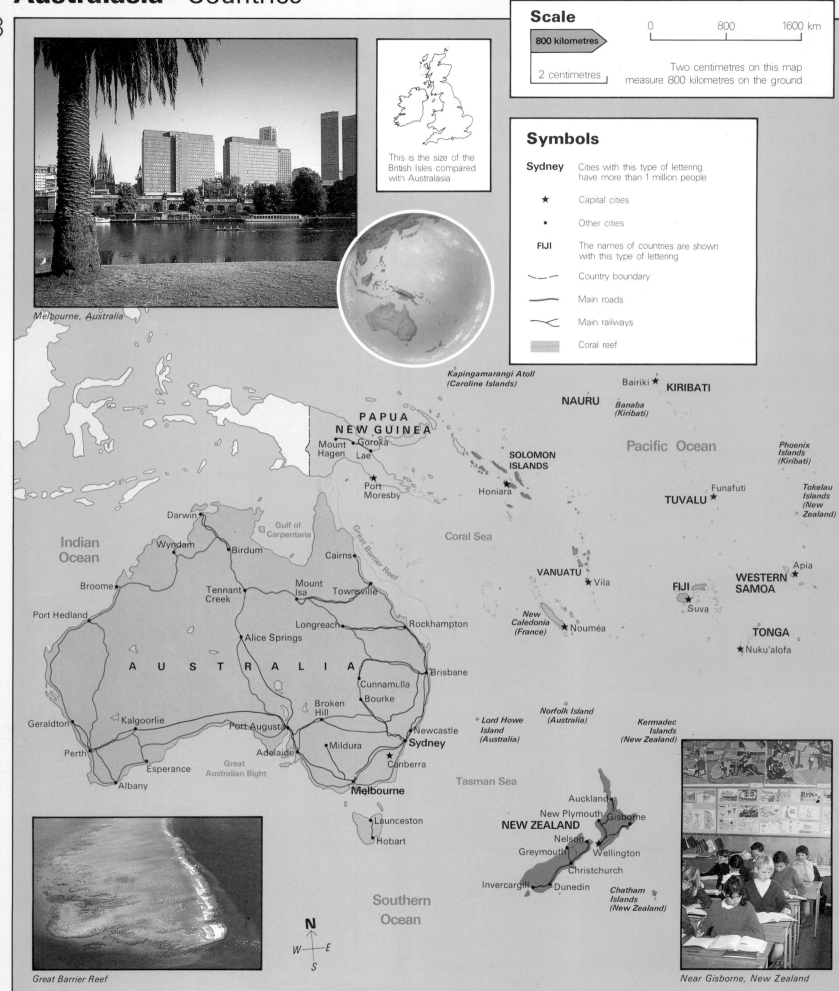

Melbourne, Australia

This is the size of the British Isles compared with Australasia

Scale

800 kilometres

2 centimetres

| 0 | 800 | 1600 km |

Two centimetres on this map measure 800 kilometres on the ground

Symbols

Sydney — Cities with this type of lettering have more than 1 million people

★ — Capital cities

• — Other cities

FIJI — The names of countries are shown with this type of lettering

⌐ — Country boundary

— — Main roads

— — Main railways

— Coral reef

Kapingamarangi Atoll (Caroline Islands)

Bairiki ★ KIRIBATI

NAURU

Banaba (Kiribati)

PAPUA NEW GUINEA

Mount Hagen Goroka
Lae

Port Moresby

SOLOMON ISLANDS

Honiara

Pacific Ocean

Phoenix Islands (Kiribati)

Funafuti
TUVALU ★

Tokelau Islands (New Zealand)

Darwin

Gulf of Carpentaria

Great Barrier Reef

Coral Sea

VANUATU
★ Vila

FIJI
★
Suva

Apia
★
WESTERN SAMOA

Indian Ocean

Wyndam Birdum

Cairns

New Caledonia (France)
★ Nouméa

TONGA
★ Nuku'alofa

Broome

Tennant Creek

Mount Isa Townsville

Port Hedland

Longreach

Rockhampton

A U S T R A L I A

Alice Springs

Brisbane

Cunnamulla

Bourke

Geraldton

Kalgoorlie

Broken Hill

Lord Howe Island (Australia)

Norfolk Island (Australia)

Kermadec Islands (New Zealand)

Perth

Port Augusta

Newcastle

Sydney ★ Canberra

Esperance

Adelaide

Mildura

Great Australian Bight

Albany

Melbourne

Tasman Sea

Auckland

New Plymouth Gisborne

NEW ZEALAND
Nelson

Launceston

Greymouth Wellington

Hobart

Christchurch

Invercargill Dunedin

Chatham Islands (New Zealand)

Southern Ocean

N
W E
S

Great Barrier Reef

Near Gisborne, New Zealand

Scale

800 kilometres

2 centimetres

0   800   1600 km

Two centimetres on this map
measure 800 kilometres on the ground

Environments

Deserts: sand, stones, short grass or shrubs

Mountains: high peaks and valleys

Warm forests: deciduous trees mixed with
coniferous trees

Hot forests: tall, lush trees and plants

Farmland: land used for growing crops

Grazing land: land used for keeping animals

▲ Highest peaks with heights given in metres

Lakes

Largest rivers

Northern Territory, Australia

Victoria, Australia

Northern Territory, Australia

*New South Wales,
Australia*

Victoria, Australia

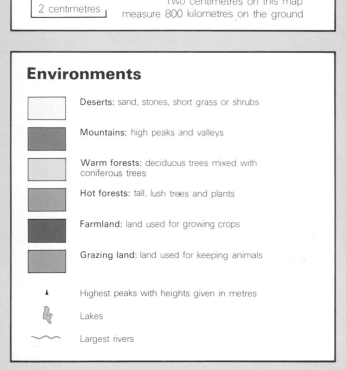

Great Sandy
Desert

*MACDONNELL
RANGES*

Simpson
Desert

Mt. Bruce
▲1226m

Gibson
Desert

▲860m
Ayers Rock

Sturt
Desert

HAMERSLEY RANGE

Great Victoria
Desert

Lake Eyre

Darling

G R E A T   D I V I D I N G   R A N G E

Murray

▲2230m
Mt. Kosciusko

Tasmania

North
Island

South
Island

▲3764m
Mt. Cook

N
W   E
S

Scale

800 kilometres

2 centimetres

0   800   1600 km

Two centimetres on this map
measure 800 kilometres on the ground

× North Pole

Bering Sea

Arctic Ocean

Aleutian Islands (U.S.A.)

Alaska (U.S.A.)

Beaufort Sea

Jan Mayen (Norway)

GREENLAND
(Denmark)

Baffin Bay

• Fairbanks
• Anchorage
Seward •
Inuvik •

Arctic Circle

Pacific Ocean

Prince Rupert •

• Yellowknife
Hay River •

C A N A D A

Hudson Bay

★ Nuuk

Vancouver •
Seattle •
Portland •

• Edmonton

• Churchill

Schefferville •

Calgary •

Regina •

Winnipeg •

• Moosonee

Sept Îles •

• St. John's

San Francisco •

Salt Lake City •

Minneapolis

Sudbury •
Ottawa ★
• Québec
Montréal

Sydney •

St. Pierre & Miquelon (France)

Las Vegas •

Denver •

Chicago •
Detroit •

Toronto •
Buffalo •
Cleveland •

Boston •

Halifax •

Los Angeles •

U N I T E D

Kansas City •

S T A T E S

Baltimore •
Washington D.C. •

New York •
Philadelphia •

San Diego •
Phoenix •
Tucson •

El Paso •

O F

St. Louis •

A M E R I C A

Memphis •

Symbols

Miami   Cities with this type of lettering have more than 1 million people

★   Capital cities

•   Other cities

CUBA   The names of countries are shown with this type of lettering

‒‒‒   Country boundary

——   Main roads

∿   Main railways

Gulf of California

Dallas •

Houston •

Atlanta •

Bermuda (U.K.)

San Antonio •

Jacksonville •

New Orleans •

Tampa •

Atlantic Ocean

Monterrey •

Gulf of Mexico

Miami •

Nassau ★

M E X I C O

Guadalajara •

Havana ★

BAHAMAS

Mexico City ★

CUBA

Santiago de Cuba •

DOMINICAN REPUBLIC

San Juan •

★

BELIZE
★ Belmopan

JAMAICA
Kingston •

HAITI
Port-au-
Prince ★

PUERTO RICO

Santo
Domingo ★

Guadeloupe (France)

GUATEMALA
Guatemala ★
San Salvador ★
EL SALVADOR

HONDURAS
★ Tegucigalpa

NICARAGUA

Caribbean Sea

DOMINICA

Martinique (France)

Netherlands Antilles (Neths.)

BARBADOS

Managua ★

Panama Canal Zone

San José ★

COSTA RICA

Panama ★

PANAMA

Port of Spain ★
TRINIDAD AND TOBAGO

Cocos Islands (Costa Rica)

This is the size of the British Isles compared with North America

Scale

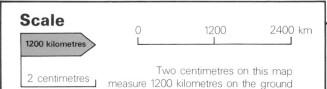

1200 kilometres

2 centimetres

0   1200   2400 km

Two centimetres on this map measure 1200 kilometres on the ground

Environments

▢	**Tundra:** frozen land
▢	**Cold forests:** mostly coniferous trees
▢	**Deserts:** sand, stones, short grass or shrubs
▢	**Mountains:** high peaks and valleys
▢	**Marsh:** land under water
▢	**Warm forests:** deciduous trees mixed with coniferous trees
▢	**Hot forests:** tall, lush trees and plants
▢	**Farmland:** land used for growing crops
▢	**Grazing land:** land used for keeping animals
▲	Highest peaks with heights given in metres
	Lakes
〰	Largest rivers

▲6187 m Mt. McKinley

▲6050 m Mt. Logan

Great Bear Lake

Great Slave Lake

Baffin Island

ROCKY MOUNTAINS

Newfoundland

Prairies

The Great Lakes

St. Lawrence

4418 m ▲ Mt. Whitney

Colorado

Missouri

APPALACHIANS

Mississippi

SIERRA MADRE

5700 m Citlaltepetl

United States of America

Kansas, United States of America

Hudson Bay, Canada

Alberta, Canada

United States of America

Scale

800 kilometres

2 centimetres

0   800   1600 km

Two centimetres on this map
measure 800 kilometres on the ground

North
Atlantic
Ocean

N
W   E
S

Caribbean Sea

Santa
Marta
Barranquilla
Cartagena
Caracas
Barcelona
Ciudad Guayana
Ciudad Bolívar
VENEZUELA
Georgetown
Paramaribo
GUYANA
Cayenne
Medellín
SURINAM
Oiapoque
Bogotá
FRENCH
GUIANA
Buenaventura
Boa Vista
Cali
COLOMBIA
Macapá
Quito
Belém
São Luís
Equator
Manaus
Santarém
Fortaleza
ECUADOR
Teresina
Natal
Guayaquil
Galapagos Islands
(Ecuador)
Iquitos
B   R   A   Z   I   L
João Pessoa
Recife
Porto Velho
Pucallpa
Aracaju
PERU
Salvador
Lima
Cuzco
Cuiabá
Brasilia
Pacific
Ocean
Goiânia
Arequipa
La Paz
Santa Cruz
Belo Horizonte
Arica
BOLIVIA
Uberaba
Vitória
Iquique
Rio de Janeiro
PARAGUAY
Antofagasta
Asunción
São Paulo
Salta
Curitiba

Symbols

Lima   Cities with this type of lettering
          have more than 1 million people

★   Capital cities

•   Other cities

PERU   The names of countries are shown
          with this type of lettering

⌣   Country boundary

—   Main roads

⌇   Main railways

Pôrto Alegre

Córdoba
Mendoza
URUGUAY
Valparaíso
Santiago
Buenos
Aires
Montevideo

South
Atlantic
Ocean

Concepción
ARGENTINA
Mar del Plata
Bahia Blanca

Puerto Montt

Comodoro Rivadavia

Juan Fernandez
Islands (Chile)

Stanley
Falkland Islands
(U.K.)

Punta Arenas

South
Georgia
(U.K.)

This is the size of the
British Isles compared
with South America

Southern Ocean

South Orkney
Islands

South
Shetland
Islands

Antarctic
Peninsula

Antarctic Circle

Scale

1200 kilometres
2 centimetres

0   1200   2400 km

Two centimetres on this map
measure 1200 kilometres on the ground

Environments

Deserts: sand, stones, short grass or shrubs.

Mountains: high peaks and valleys.

Marsh: land under water.

Warm forests: deciduous trees mixed with coniferous trees.

Hot forests: tall, lush trees and plants.

Savanna: tall, thick grasses.

Farmland: land used for growing crops.

Grazing land: land used for keeping animals.

▲ Highest peaks with height given in metres

Lakes

Largest rivers

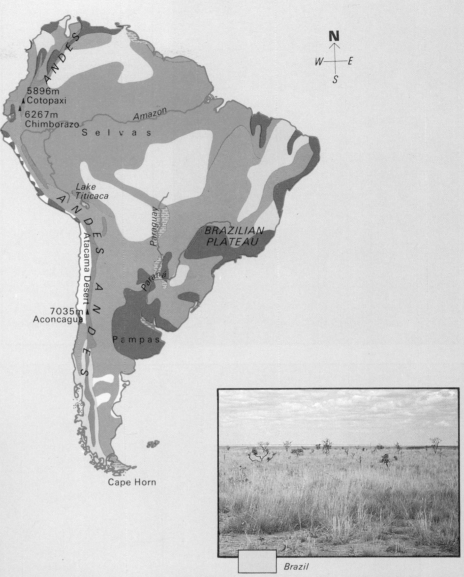

ANDES

5896m
▲ Cotopaxi
6267m
Chimborazo

Amazon

Selvas

Lake
Titicaca

Paraguay

BRAZILIAN
PLATEAU

Paraná

ANDES

Atacama Desert

7035m ▲
Aconcagua

Pampas

Cape Horn

N
W — E
S

Bolivia

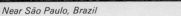

Near São Paulo, Brazil

Near São Paulo, Brazil

Brazil

Near Porto Velho, Brazil

The Caribbean

St. George's, Grenada

Symbols

⌇	country boundary
〰	motorways and main roads
⌁	main railways
⌂	canal
✈	international airport
〜	river
🗾	lake
▲	peak or highest point

Towns

■	largest (with more than 1 million people)
●	large (with more than 100,000 people but less than 1 million people)
•	others (with less than 100,000 people)

Scale

400 kilometres

2 centimetres

0   400   800 km

Two centimetres on this map measure 400 kilometres on the ground

Land Height

Measured above Sea Level

▓	More than 2000 metres
▒	1000 – 2000 metres
░	500 – 1000 metres
░	200 – 500 metres
░	Less than 200 metres

Barbados

Austin
San Antonio
Nuevo Laredo
Houston
U.S.A.
Jackson
Baton Rouge
Birmingham
Atlanta
Columbia
Corpus Christi
Mobile
New Orleans
Savannah
Matamoros
Jacksonville
Tampico
Tampa
Cape Canaveral
Gulf of Mexico
Veracruz
Palm Beach
Miami
Grand Bahama
Great Abaco
Mérida
Yucatan Peninsula
Straits of Florida
Nassau
Andros
Eleuthera
Cat
MEXICO
Yucatan Channel
Havana
Santa Clara
BAHAMAS
Long
CUBA
Camagüey
Acklins
Caicos Islands
Cayman Islands
Holguín
Great Inagua
Belize
Belmopan
Greater
Santiago de Cuba
Guantánamo
DOMINICAN REPUBLIC
Atlantic Ocean
GUATEMALA
BELIZE
JAMAICA
HAITI
Santiago
San Juan
Virgin Islands
Guatemala
San Pedro de Sula
Kingston
Port-au-Prince
Santo Domingo
Anguilla
San Salvador
HONDURAS
PUERTO RICO
St Kitts
Barbuda
EL SALVADOR
Tegucigalpa
Antilles
Nevis
Antigua
Guadeloupe
NICARAGUA
Antilles
Dominica
Managua
Caribbean Sea
Mt. Pelée 1463 m
Lake Nicaragua
Martinique
St. Lucia
Pacific Ocean
St. Vincent
Barbados
COSTA RICA
San José
Aruba
Curaçao
Grenada
Santa Marta
Bonaire
Margarita
Tobago
Panama Canal
Barranquilla
Cartagena
Maracaibo
Valencia
Caracas
Port of Spain
PANAMA
Panamá
Magdalena
Lake Maracaibo
Barquisimeto
Cumaná
Trinidad
Cauca
Cúcuta
San Cristóbal
VENEZUELA
Ciudad Guayana
COLOMBIA
Bucaramanga
Orinoco
Ciudad Bolívar
GUYANA

N
W   E
S

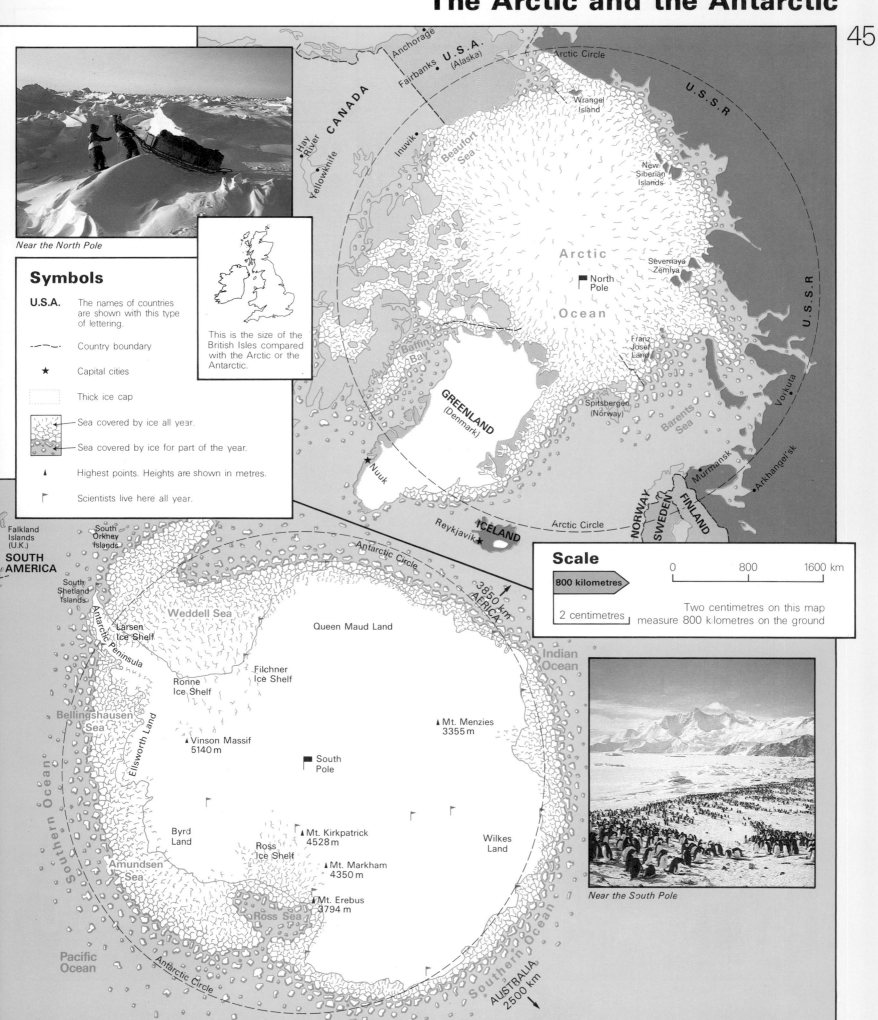

Near the North Pole

Symbols

U.S.A.   The names of countries are shown with this type of lettering.

– – –   Country boundary

★   Capital cities

Thick ice cap

Sea covered by ice all year.

Sea covered by ice for part of the year.

▲   Highest points. Heights are shown in metres.

⌐   Scientists live here all year.

This is the size of the British Isles compared with the Arctic or the Antarctic.

Scale

800 kilometres

2 centimetres

0   800   1600 km

Two centimetres on this map measure 800 kilometres on the ground

Near the South Pole

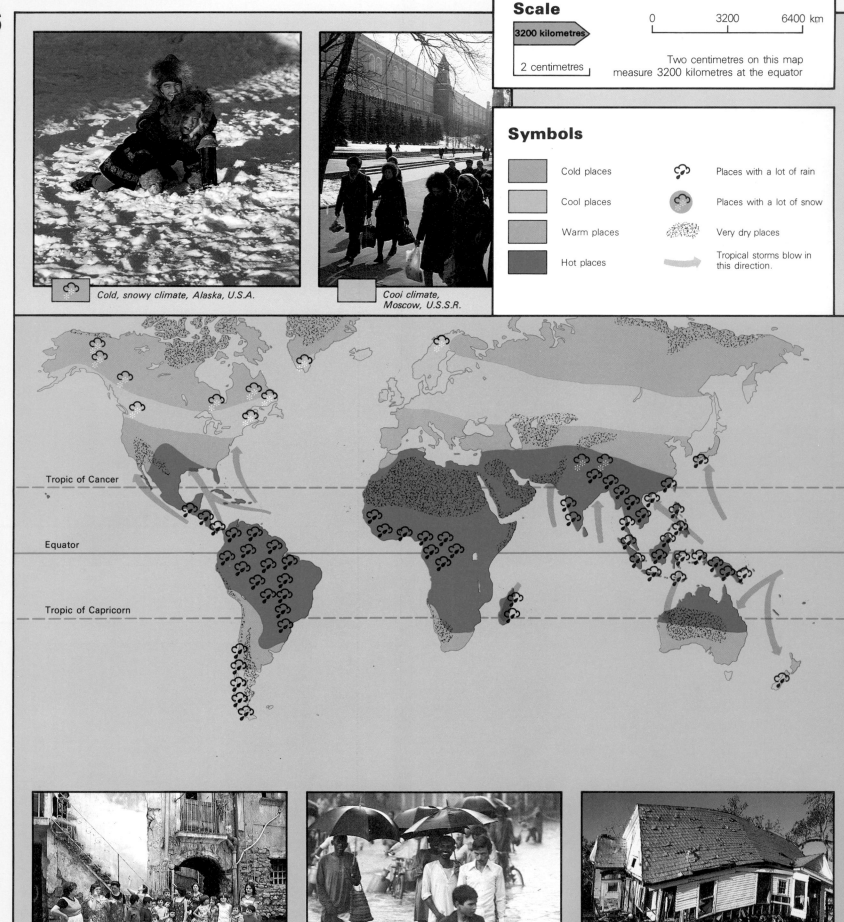

Scale

3200 kilometres

2 centimetres

0   3200   6400 km

Two centimetres on this map
measure 3200 kilometres at the equator

Symbols

Cold places

Cool places

Warm places

Hot places

Places with a lot of rain

Places with a lot of snow

Very dry places

Tropical storms blow in
this direction.

Cold, snowy climate, Alaska, U.S.A.

Cool climate,
Moscow, U.S.S.R.

Tropic of Cancer

Equator

Tropic of Capricorn

Warm climate, Italy

Hot wet climate, India

Storm damage, Louisiana, U.S.A.

Scale

3200 kilometres

2 centimetres

0   3200   6400 km

Two centimetres on this map
measure 3200 kilometres at the equator

Edwards Air Force Base, U.S.A.

Amy Johnson

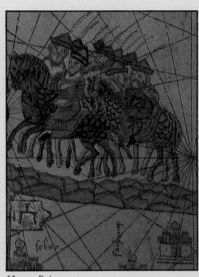

Marco Polo

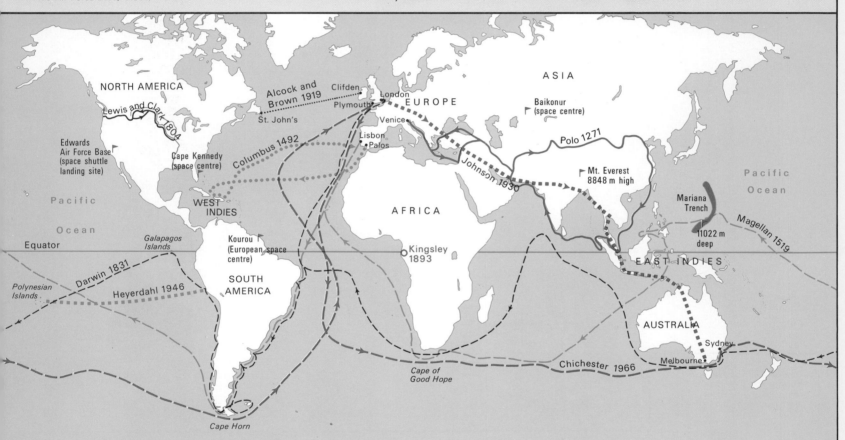

Great Adventures

Only a few of the world's great adventures are
shown here. There are many more.

— **Marco Polo** Tells people in Europe
about the riches of the East.

••••••• **Christopher Columbus** Discovers
the West Indies.

– – – **Ferdinand Magellan** First journey
round the world

— **M. Lewis and W. Clark** Explored from
the river Missouri to the Pacific Ocean.

– – – **Charles Darwin** A voyage in the
Beagle to study plants and animals.

○ **Mary Kingsley** Victorian lady
explores West Africa.

•••••••••• **J. Alcock and A. Brown** First
non-stop flight across the Atlantic.

••••••• **Amy Johnson** First woman to fly
to Australia.

•• •• •• **Thor Heyerdahl** Peru to Polynesia
in the *Kon-Tiki* raft.

– •– •– **Francis Chichester** Record-breaking
round-the-world yachtsman.

Ⰶ Some other great adventures took place
here.

World People

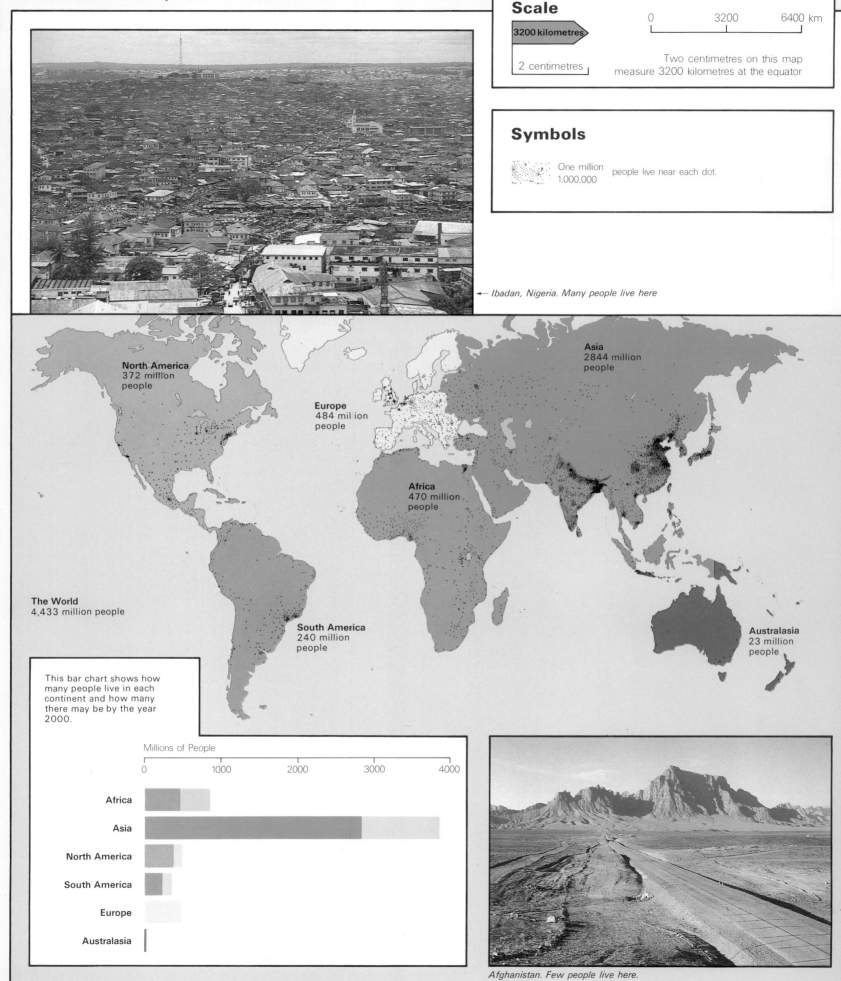

Scale

3200 kilometres

2 centimetres

0   3200   6400 km

Two centimetres on this map
measure 3200 kilometres at the equator

Symbols

One million
1,000,000   people live near each dot.

← *Ibadan, Nigeria. Many people live here*

North America
372 million
people

Europe
484 million
people

Asia
2844 million
people

Africa
470 million
people

The World
4,433 million people

South America
240 million
people

Australasia
23 million
people

This bar chart shows how
many people live in each
continent and how many
there may be by the year
2000.

Millions of People

	0	1000	2000	3000	4000

Africa

Asia

North America

South America

Europe

Australasia

Afghanistan. Few people live here.

Scale

3200 kilometres

2 centimetres

0   3200   6400 km

Two centimetres on this map
measure 3200 kilometres at the equator

Welfare

Some people in the world are rich. Many people are poor
or hungry or suffering as a result of war.

Rich countries This colour shows the 25 richest
countries in the world. Not everyone in these countries
is rich but most live comfortably.

Poor countries This colour shows the 40 poorest
countries in the world. Not everyone in these countries
is poor but most are in need.

War This symbol shows places where there has
recently been a war.

Famine This symbol shows places where there has
recently been a shortage of food.

Ghana

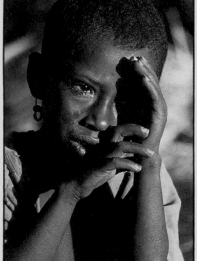
Ethiopia

Lebanon

West Germany

World Food

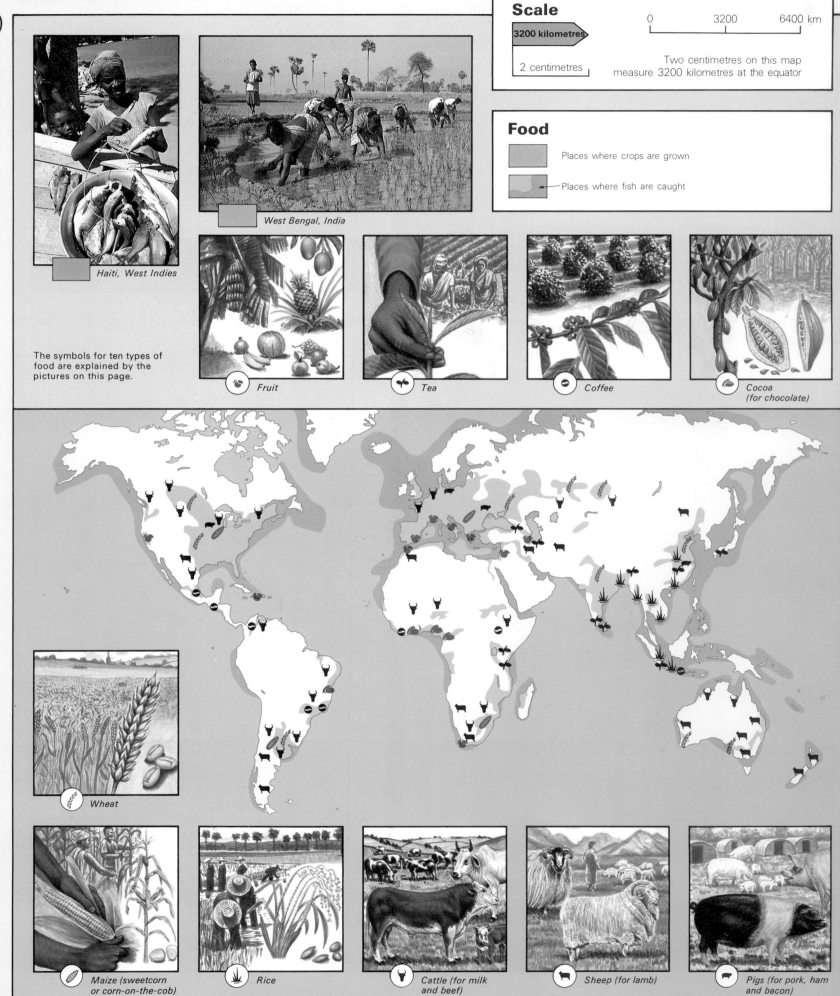

Scale

3200 kilometres

2 centimetres

0   3200   6400 km

Two centimetres on this map measure 3200 kilometres at the equator

Food

Places where crops are grown

Places where fish are caught

Haiti, West Indies

West Bengal, India

The symbols for ten types of food are explained by the pictures on this page.

🍐 *Fruit*

🦟 *Tea*

⬤ *Coffee*

⬤ *Cocoa (for chocolate)*

🌾 *Wheat*

🌽 *Maize (sweetcorn or corn-on-the-cob)*

🌿 *Rice*

🐂 *Cattle (for milk and beef)*

🐑 *Sheep (for lamb)*

🐖 *Pigs (for pork, ham and bacon)*

Scale

3200 kilometres

2 centimetres

0   3200   6400 km

Two centimetres on this map
measure 3200 kilometres at the equator

Raw Materials

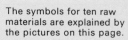

Places where there are
many factories that make
things from raw materials.

The symbols for ten raw
materials are explained by
the pictures on this page.

Oil (to make plastic, nylon, petrol
and other things)

Coal

Iron (to make steel)

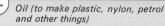

Copper

Gold

Bauxite (to make aluminium)

Timber (for wood and
making paper)

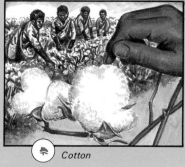

Cotton

Rubber

Wool

Use this gazetteer to find large towns, high land and rivers in the British Isles. You will find each place on the pages shown below. Look for the area where the columns (shown by letters) and the rows (shown by numbers) meet.

Belfast	Towns are shown in this colour
Thames	Rivers are shown in this colour
Exmoor	High land is shown in this colour
15	Page numbers are shown like this
J6	Column letters and row numbers are shown like this

Use the map on page 10 to find counties, regions and districts in the British Isles.

A
Aberdeen, Grampian 18 **J9**
Aire, England 16 **J5**
Antrim Mountains, Northern Ireland 19 **E7**
Avon, Avon/Wiltshire 13 **J3**
Avon, Warwickshire 16 **K4**
Ayr, Strathclyde 18 **G7**

B
Banbury, Oxfordshire 14 **K4**
Bangor, Northern Ireland 19 **F6**
Barking, Greater London 14 **M3**
Barnet, Greater London 14 **L3**
Barnsley, South Yorkshire 16 **K5**
Barrow, Irish Republic 19 **E4**
Barrow-in-Furness, Cumbria 17 **H6**
Basildon, Essex 14 **M3**
Basingstoke, Hampshire 14 **K3**
Bath, Avon 13 **J3**
Bebington, Merseyside 16 **H5**
Bedford, Bedfordshire 14 **L4**
Belfast, Northern Ireland 19 **E6**
Benfleet, Essex 14 **M3**
Ben Nevis, Highland 18 **G8**
Bexley, Greater London 14 **M3**
Birkenhead, Merseyside 16 **H5**
Blackpool, Lancashire 16 **H5**
Blackwater, Irish Republic 19 **C4**
Bolton, Greater Manchester 16 **J5**
Bootle, Merseyside 16 **H5**
Bournemouth, Dorset 13 **J2**
Bradford, West Yorkshire 16 **K5**
Brecon Beacons, Wales 15 **H3**
Brent, Greater London 14 **L3**
Brentwood, Essex 14 **M3**
Brighton, West Sussex 14 **L2**
Bristol, Avon 13 **J3**
Bromley, Greater London 14 **M3**
Burnley, Lancashire 16 **J5**
Bury, Greater Manchester 16 **J5**

C
Cader Idris, Gwynedd 15 **H4**
Cairngorms, Scotland 18 **H9**
Camberley, Surrey 14 **L3**
Cambrian Mountains, Wales 15 **H4**
Cambridge, Cambridgeshire 14 **M4**
Cannock, Staffordshire 16 **J4**
Canterbury, Kent 14 **N3**
Cardiff, South Glamorgan 15 **H3**
Carlisle, Cumbria 17 **H6**
Carn Eige, Highland 18 **F9**
Carrauntoohill, Kerry 19 **B3**
Chatham, Kent 14 **M3**
Cheadle, Greater Manchester 16 **J5**
Chelmsford, Essex 14 **M3**
Cheltenham, Gloucestershire 13 **J3**
Chester, Cheshire 16 **J5**
Chesterfield, Derbyshire 16 **K5**
Cheviot Hills, Scotland/England 17 **J7**
Chiltern Hills, England 14 **L3**
Chorley, Lancashire 16 **J5**
Clyde, Strathclyde 18 **H7**
Clydebank, Strathclyde 18 **G7**
Coatbridge, Strathclyde 18 **G7**
Colchester, Essex 14 **M3**
Cork, Cork 19 **C3**
Cotswold Hills, England 13 **J3**
Coventry, Warwickshire 16 **K4**
Crawley, West Sussex 14 **L3**
Crewe, Cheshire 16 **J5**
Crosby, Merseyside 16 **H5**
Croydon, Greater London 14 **L3**
Cwmbran, Gwent 15 **J3**

D
Darlington, Durham 17 **K6**
Dartmoor, Devon 13 **H2**
Dee, Grampian 18 **J9**
Derby, Derbyshire 16 **K4**
Doncaster, South Yorkshire 16 **K5**
Douglas, Isle of Man 17 **G6**
Dove, England 16 **K5**
Dover, Kent 14 **N3**
Dublin, Dublin 19 **E5**
Dudley, West Midlands 16 **J4**
Dundee, Tayside 18 **H8**
Dunfermline, Fife 18 **H8**
Dunkery Beacon, Somerset 13 **H3**
Dun Laoghaire, Dublin 19 **E5**
Durham, Durham 17 **K6**

E
Ealing, Greater London 14 **L3**
Eastbourne, East Susex 14 **M2**
East Kilbride, Strathclyde 18 **G7**
Eastleigh, Hampshire 14 **K2**
Edinburgh, Lothian 18 **H7**
Ellesmere Port, Cheshire 16 **J5**
Enfield, Greater London 14 **L3**
Epsom, Surrey 14 **L3**
Erne, Ireland 19 **C6**
Exe, England 13 **H3**
Exeter, Devon 13 **H2**
Exmoor, England 13 **H3**

F
Falkirk, Central 18 **H7**
Fareham, Hampshire 14 **K2**
Farnborough, Surrey 14 **L3**
Folkestone, Kent 14 **N3**
Forth, Scotland 18 **G8**

G
Gateshead, Tyne and Wear 17 **K6**
Gillingham, Kent 14 **M3**
Glasgow, Strathclyde 18 **G7**
Gloucester, Gloucestershire 13 **J3**
Gosport, Hampshire 14 **K2**
Grampian Mountains, Scotland 18 **G8**
Grangemouth, Central 17 **H8**
Gravesend, Kent 14 **M3**
Grays, Essex 14 **M3**
Great Malvern, Hereford and Worcester 16 **J4**
Great Ouse, England 14 **L4**
Great Yarmouth, Norfolk 14 **N4**
Greenock, Strathclyde 18 **F7**
Greenwich, Greater London 14 **M3**
Grimsby, Humberside 16 **L5**
Guildford, Surrey 14 **L3**

H
Halesowen, West Midlands 16 **J4**
Halifax, West Yorkshire 16 **K5**
Hamilton, Strathclyde 18 **G7**
Harlow, Essex 14 **M3**
Harrogate, West Yorkshire 16 **K5**
Harrow, Greater London 14 **L3**
Hartlepool, Cleveland 17 **K6**
Hastings, East Sussex 14 **M2**
Havant, Hampshire 14 **L2**
Hay-on-Wye, Hereford and Worcester 15 **H4**
Haywards Heath, West Sussex 14 **L2**
Helvellyn, Cumbria 17 **J6**
Hemel Hempstead, Hertfordshire 14 **L3**
Hereford, Hereford and Worcester 15 **J4**
High Wycombe, Buckinghamshire 14 **L3**
Hillingdon, Greater London 14 **L3**
Hinckley, Leicestershire 16 **K4**
Hounslow, Greater London 14 **L3**
Hove, West Sussex 14 **L2**
Huddersfield, West Yorkshire 16 **K5**
Humber, Humberside 16 **L5**
Hyde, Greater Manchester 16 **J5**

I
Ingleborough, North Yorkshire 16 **J6**
Inverness, Highland 18 **G9**
Ipswich, Suffolk 14 **N4**

K
Keighley, West Yorkshire 16 **K5**
Kidderminster, Hereford and Worcester 16 **J4**
Kilmarnock, Strathclyde 18 **G7**
Kinder Scout, Derbyshire 16 **K5**
Kingston, Greater London 14 **L3**
Kingston-upon-Hull, Humberside 16 **L5**
Kirkby, Merseyside 16 **J5**
Kirkwall, Orkney Islands 18 **J10**

L
Lake District, England 17 **H6**
Leeds, West Yorkshire 16 **K5**
Leicester, Leicestershire 16 **K4**
Lerwick, Shetland Islands 18 **J12**
Limerick, Limerick 19 **C4**
Lincoln, Lincolnshire 16 **L5**
Liverpool, Merseyside 16 **J5**
Llanfairfechan, Gwynedd 15 **H5**
London, Greater London 14 **L3**
Londonderry, Northern Ireland 19 **D6**
Longbenton, Tyne and Wear 17 **K7**
Lowestoft, Suffolk 14 **N4**
Luton, Bedfordshire 14 **L3**

M
Maidenhead, Berkshire 14 **L3**
Maidstone, Kent 14 **M3**
Manchester, Greater Manchester 16 **J5**
Mansfield, Nottinghamshire 16 **K5**
Margate, Kent 14 **N3**
Medway, England 14 **M3**
Mersey, England 16 **J5**
Merton, Greater London 14 **L3**
Merthyr Tydfil, Mid Glamorgan 15 **H3**
Mickle Fell, England 17 **J6**
Middlesbrough, Cleveland 17 **K6**
Middleton, Greater Manchester 16 **J5**
Milton Keynes, Buckinghamshire 14 **L4**

N
Nelson, Lancashire 16 **J5**
Newcastle-under-Lyme, Staffordshire 16 **J5**
Newcastle-upon-Tyne, Tyne and Wear 17 **K6**
Newport, Gwent 15 **J3**
Newtownabbey, Northern Ireland 19 **E6**
Newtownards, Northern Ireland 19 **F6**
Northampton, Northamptonshire 14 **L4**
North Downs, Kent 14 **M3**
Northwest Highlands, Scotland 18 **F9**
North York Moors, North Yorkshire 16 **L6**
Norwich, Norfolk 14 **N4**
Nottingham, Nottinghamshire 16 **K4**
Nuneaton, Warwickshire 16 **K4**

O
Oakham, Leicestershire 16 **L4**
Oldham, Greater Manchester 16 **J5**
Ouse, North Yorkshire 16 **K5**
Oxford, Oxfordshire 14 **K3**

P
Paisley, Strathclyde 18 **G7**
Pennines, England 16/17 **J6**
Peterborough, Cambridgeshire 14 **L4**
Plymouth, Devon 13 **G2**
Poole, Dorset 13 **K2**
Portsmouth, Hampshire 14 **K2**
Port Talbot, West Glamorgan 15 **H3**
Preston, Lancashire 16 **J5**

R
Ramsgate, Kent 14 **N3**
Reading, Berkshire 14 **K3**
Redbridge, Greater London 14 **M3**
Redcar, Cleveland 17 **K6**
Redditch, Hereford and Worcester 16 **K4**
Reigate, Surrey 14 **L3**
Rhondda, Mid Glamorgan 15 **H3**
Richmond, Greater London 14 **L3**
Rochdale, Greater Manchester 16 **J5**
Rochester, Kent 14 **M3**
Rotherham, South Yorkshire 16 **K5**
Rugby, Warwickshire 16 **K4**
Runcorn, Cheshire 16 **J5**

S
Sale, Greater Manchester 16 **J5**
Salford, Greater Manchester 16 **J5**
Salisbury, Wiltshire 13 **K3**
Salisbury Plain, Wiltshire 13 **K3**
Sawel, North Ireland 19 **D6**
Scafell Pike, Cumbria 17 **H6**
Scarborough, North Yorkshire 16 **L6**
Scunthorpe, Lincolnshire 16 **L5**
Severn, Wales/England 13/15 **J3**
Shannon, Irish Republic 19 **C4**
Sheffield, South Yorkshire 16 **K5**
Shrewsbury, Shropshire 16 **J4**
Skipton, North Yorkshire 16 **J5**

Slough, Buckinghamshire 14 **L3**
Snowdon, Gwynedd 15 **G5**
Solihull, West Midlands 16 **K4**
Southampton, Hampshire 14 **K2**
South Downs, England 14 **L2**
Southend-on-Sea, Essex 14 **M3**
Southern Uplands, Scotland 18 **H7**
Southport, Merseyside 16 **H5**
South Shields, Tyne and Wear 17 **K6**
Spey, Scotland 18 **H9**
Stafford, Staffordshire 16 **J4**
Staines, Surrey 14 **L3**
St. Albans, Hertfordshire 14 **L3**
St. Andrews, Fife 18 **J8**
Stevenage, Hertfordshire 14 **L3**
St. Helens, Merseyside 16 **J5**
Stirling, Central 18 **G8**
Stockport, Greater Manchester 16 **J5**
Stockton-on-Tees, Cleveland 17 **K6**
Stoke-on-Trent, Staffordshire 16 **J4**
Stourbridge, West Midlands 16 **J4**
Sunderland, Tyne and Wear 17 **K6**
Sutton, Greater London 14 **L3**
Sutton Coldfield, West Midlands 16 **K4**
Swansea, West Glamorgan 15 **G3**
Swindon, Wiltshire 13 **K3**

T
Tamar, Devon/Cornwall 13 **G2**
Tamworth, Staffordshire 16 **K4**
Tay, Tayside 18 **H8**
Tees, England 17 **J6**
Telford, Shropshire 16 **J4**
Thames, England 14 **K3**
The Weald, England 14 **M3**
Torbay, Devon 13 **H2**
Trent, England 16 **K4**
Truro, Cornwall 13 **F2**
Tryfan, Wales 15 **H5**
Tweed, Borders 18 **J7**
Tyne, England 17 **J7**
Tynemouth, Tyne and Wear 17 **K7**
Tywi, Dyfed 15 **H3**

U Usk, Wales 15 **H3**

W
Wakefield, West Yorkshire 16 **K5**
Wallasey, Merseyside 16 **H5**
Walsall, West Midlands 16 **K4**
Warley, West Midlands 16 **J4**
Warrington, Cheshire 16 **J5**
Washington, Tyne and Wear 17 **K6**
Watford, Hertfordshire 14 **L3**
West Bromwich, West Midlands 16 **J4**
Weston-super-Mare, Avon 13 **J3**
Weymouth, Dorset 13 **J2**
Whitby, North Yorkshire 16 **L6**
Wicklow Mountains, Irish Republic 19 **E4**
Widnes, Cheshire 16 **J5**
Wigan, Greater Manchester 16 **J5**
Winchester, Hampshire 14 **K3**
Windsor, Berkshire 14 **L3**
Wolverhampton, West Midlands 16 **J4**
Worcester, Hereford and Worcester 16 **J4**
Worthing, West Sussex 14 **L2**
Wrexham, Clwyd 15 **H5**
Wye, Wales/England 13/15 **J3**

Y Yes Tor, Devon 13 **H2**
York, North Yorkshire 16 **K5**